MALTIPOO BIBLE AND MALTIPOOS
Your Perfect Maltipoo Guide

Maltipoo, Maltipoos, Maltipoo Puppies,
Maltipoo Dogs, Maltipoo Breeders, Maltipoo Care,
Maltipoo Training, Health, Behavior, Grooming,
Breeding, History and More!

By Matthew Masterson

© DYM Worldwide Publishers, 2020.

Published by DYM Worldwide Publishers 2020.

ISBN: 978-1-913154-24-0

Copyright © DYM Worldwide Publishers, 2020.
2 Lansdowne Row, Number 240 London W1J 6HL

ALL RIGHTS RESERVED. This book contains material protected under International & Federal Copyright Laws & Treaties. Any unauthorized reprint or use of this material is strictly prohibited. No part of this book may be reproduced or transmitted in any form or by any means, electronic, mechanical, or otherwise, including photocopying or recording, or by any information storage or retrieval system without express written permission from the author.

Copyright and Trademarks. This publication is Copyright 2020 by DYM Worldwide Publishers. All products, publications, software, and services mentioned and recommended in this publication are protected by trademarks. In such an instance, all trademarks & copyright belonging to the respective owners.

All rights reserved. No part of this book may be reproduced or transferred in any form or by any means, graphic, electronic, or mechanical, including but not limited to photocopying, recording, taping, scanning, or by any information storage retrieval system, without the written permission of the author. Pictures used in this book are royalty-free pictures purchased from stock photo websites with full rights for use within this work.

Disclaimer and Legal Notice. This product is not legal or medical advice and should not be interpreted in that manner. You need to do your own due diligence to determine if the content of this product is right for you. The author, publisher, distributors, and or/affiliates of this product are not liable for any damages or losses associated with the content in this product. While every attempt has been made to verify the information shared in this publication, neither the author, publisher, distributors, and/or affiliates assume any responsibility for errors, omissions, or contrary interpretation of the subject matter herein. Any perceived slights to any specific person(s) or organization(s) are purely unintentional. We have no control over the nature, content, and availability of the websites listed in this book.

The inclusion of any website links does not necessarily imply a recommendation or endorse the views expressed within them. DYM Worldwide Publishers takes no responsibility for, and will not be liable for, the websites being temporarily or being removed from the Internet. The accuracy and completeness of the information provided herein and opinions stated herein are not guaranteed or warranted to produce any particular results, and the advice or strategies contained herein may not be suitable for every individual. The author, publisher, distributors, and/or affiliates shall not be liable for any loss incurred as a consequence of the use and application, directly or indirectly, of any information presented in this work. This publication is designed to provide information regarding the subject matter covered. The information included in this book has been compiled to give an overview of the topics covered. The information contained in this book has been compiled to provide an overview of the subject. It is not intended as medical advice and should not be construed as such. For a firm diagnosis of any medical conditions, you should consult a doctor or veterinarian (as related to animal health). The writer, publisher, distributors, and/or affiliates of this work are not responsible for any damages or negative consequences following any of the treatments or methods highlighted in this book.

Website links are for informational purposes only and should not be seen as a personal endorsement; the same applies to any products or services mentioned in this work. The reader should also be aware that although the web links included were correct at the time of writing, they may become out of date in the future. Any pricing or currency exchange rate information was accurate at the time of writing but may become out of date in the future. The Author, Publisher, distributors, and/or affiliates assume no responsibility for pricing and currency exchange rates mentioned within this work.

Table of Contents

Chapter 1 – The Maltipoo: An Introduction 9
                     What is a Maltipoo? 12

Chapter 2 – Maltipoo History 15
                     Maltipoo Origins 16
                     Different "Types" of Maltipoo 17
                     Coat 21
                     A Warning About Maltipoo Crossbreeds 22

Chapter 3 – The Maltipoo Breed 25
                     Maltipoo Breed Standard 25
                     Maltipoo Breed Recognition 25

Chapter 4 – Buying a Maltipoo 31
                     Where to Get a Maltipoo? 32
                     Should You Get a Puppy or an Adult? 34
                     Maltipoo Temperament 35
                     The Maltipoo Around Others 36
                     Pros and Cons of a Maltipoo 38
                     Cons 38
                     Pros 39
                     Is it Easy to Care for? 40

Chapter 5 – Your Maltipoo Puppy 43
                     Maltipoo stages 44
                     Picking the Right Breeder 45

	How to Choose the Right Puppy? 46
	What Color to Go for? 47
	Bringing a Puppy Home 48
	Puppy-proofing the Home...49
	Puppy Spaces 51
	The First Few Days 52
	Pet Training..54

Chapter 6 – Your Pet Maltipoo 57
  Before You Get One 57
  Feeding Your Maltipoo 58
  What to Feed Your Maltipoo 59
  Homemade Dog Food..61
  A Good Balance 62
  How Often to Feed Your Maltipoo..........................63
  Your Maltipoo's Living Environment 64
  Maltipoo Living Space 64
  Other Ideal Conditions 66
  Maltipoo Socialization 66

Chapter 7 – Caring for your Maltipoo..67
  Playing and Bonding 67
  Maltipoo Exercise 70
  Walking...71
  Maltipoo Separation Anxiety 74
  Maltipoo Transport..78
  Other Things to Remember 81
  Maltipoo Toys...82

Chapter 8 – Grooming and Bathing Your Maltipoo......................83
  Keeping Your Maltipoo Clean 83
  Maltipoo "Shedding"..83

	Maltipoo Bathing	84
	Maltipoo Grooming	88
	Professional Grooming	90
	Maltipoo Care Supplies	90
	Don't Use Your Shampoo on Your Dog	92
Chapter 9 –	How to Train Your Maltipoo	93
	How Difficult are Maltipoos to Train?	93
	Equipment You Will Need	94
	What to Train Your Maltipoo	94
	Teaching Your Dog How to Sit	96
	Teaching Your Maltipoo to Stay	96
	Teaching Your Maltipoo How to Come To You	97
	Teaching Your Dog How Not to Bark	98
	Teaching Your Dog How Not to Jump at You	99
	Maltipoo Tricks	100
	Training Yourself	102
Chapter 10 –	Maltipoo Health	105
	Signs of a Healthy Maltipoo	105
	When to Be Concerned	106
	Maltipoo Lifespan	108
	Maltipoo Food Allergies	108
	Maltipoo Immunizations	110
	Medical Conditions and Their Solutions	112
	Pros and Cons of Neutering / Spaying	115
	How to Choose a Good Veterinarian For Your Maltipoo	117
Chapter 11 –	Maltipoo Breeding	119
	How to Breed the Best Maltipoo Possible	120
	Ideal Breeding Age	121

        A Few Rules 122
        Breeding for Color 123
        Signs of Pregnancy 123
        A Warning for Maltipoo Breeders 125

Chapter 12 – Caring For Older Maltipoos 127
        Signs of Aging 128
        Behavioral Changes 128
        The Daily Routine for Older Maltipoos 129
        Saying Goodbye 131
        If You Decide to Make a Painful Decision 132
        Memorializing Your Dog 133
        An Important Thing to Remember 133

Chapter 13 – Things Maltipoo Owners Must Know 135
        Maltipoo Licenses 135
        Maltipoo Insurance 136

Conclusion   139

Bonus Chapter – Your Trusted Maltipoo Resource List 143

CHAPTER 1

The Maltipoo: An Introduction

Around 14,000 years ago, ancient man first discovered that the dog was a good companion and has always kept dogs by his side ever since. At first, it was only for survival reasons; dogs helped ancient man hunt and get his food, sniffed out danger for him, and helped keep him safe from enemies at night.

As the centuries went by, life became better for men. However, he still preferred to keep his canine best friend by his side. Although the initial purpose of a dog was to keep humans alive, people found out that dogs were good for making life worth living as well.

The Maltipoo is one of the most rewarding crossbreeds to own!

Dog breeders began to breed different dogs to suit different kinds of people and their various needs and quirks. Big, active dogs were bred for keeping up with people with active lifestyles. Small designer dogs went to those who wanted animals that could also serve as fashion statements. The tough dogs were trained for jobs in the police and military that humans were not capable of doing, and so on.

Breeding two different species of dogs produced a unique breed. And taking that result and breeding it with another produces an even more unique breed. With that, breeders found out they could provide dogs with the good qualities that they wanted and none of the bad characteristics, or at least as little of the bad attributes as possible.

One breed that many people are familiar with is the poodle. Today it is widely known as a show dog, but unknown to many, the poodle did not start like that. It was bred by hunters in France and Germany to be water dogs that retrieved ducks that had been shot down.

The word "poodle" is said to have been a bastardization of a Low German word "pudel" meaning "to splash in water," which is what they did to go after fallen game birds.

By the 18th century, the poodle had become the principal pet dog in Spain. Despite their apparent talents in the outdoors, they would eventually become the preferred pets of French royalty. So much so that poodles are represented in many paintings, drawings, and engravings commissioned in that era.

Over the years, the poodle was bred with other species to become smaller in size. There are now three standard sizes, as described by both the American Kennel Club (AKC) and the UK Kennel Club (KC); standard, miniature, and toy.

Contrary to popular belief, their puffball appearance (where the hair seems to concentrate "balls" on their head, upper chest, lower legs, and even the tip of their tail) is not their natural look but the result of professional trimming and grooming. By nature, poodles are covered by an even but coarse coat all over their bodies.

Poodles are described as active, agile, and very smart, owing to their past as active hunting partners.

Another breed that gained prominence was the Maltese, another dog that originated from Europe. Unlike the poodle which appears to have bred by modern humans, the Maltese go further back into history. The earliest mention of a Maltese goes back to 370 BCE when Aristotle described the breed, calling it the Malleate Catelli.

Just as the poodle was bred to retrieve game fowl, the Maltese was bred to help its human companions. This was to control rodents and rats. Its small size made it ideal to go after rats and other pests that threatened the food stores of humans living around the Mediterranean.

Eventually, it became known for its cuddliness and small size, and soon it became the favorite of Mediterranean noblewomen.

Today, the Maltese is officially recognized by the AKC as a breed in the toy dog group. They average seven to nine inches high and weigh no more than seven lbs. They have long coats that often reach the floor, and they are generally described as gentle, playful, and charming.

As a holdout to their being ridders of rodents for centuries, Maltese are alert and fearless. They also get along with other dogs and respond well to reward-based training despite showing signs of occasional stubbornness.

You can probably guess by now that these two breeds, the Maltese and the Poodle, were bred to come up with one of the cutest and cuddliest dog breeds to ever walk the earth, the Maltipoo.

What is a Maltipoo?

Cute, cuddly, and popular as they are, the Maltipoo is not considered a breed. Bodies like the AKC recognize the Poodle and the Maltese as a breed. However, they do not acknowledge the offspring of such a pairing.

It is for this reason the Maltipoo is called in kennel parlance as a crossbreed (this will be discussed more in an upcoming chapter).

However, this has not discouraged Maltipoo owners from all over the United States, the United Kingdom, and other parts of the world from loving and adoring their pets. Or from organizing themselves into clubs that specialize in this crossbreed, whether it is to buy, sell, or rescue.

It has also not stopped dog breeders from further experimenting with combining Maltipoo genes with that of other dog species to come up with even more crossbreeds.

Do you happen to own one of these dogs but aren't sure what to expect? Or do you want to get one of these dogs but have no idea what to do? This guide will teach you everything you need to know about how to get, raise, play with, and take care of your Maltipoo.

You will also learn about how to make your home friendly for Maltipoos, how to transport them safely, how to take care of them outside the house, and other things a Maltipoo owner must know.

Above all else, this book will teach you how to adopt the mindset of a Maltipoo owner. Although taking care of different types of dogs has a general outline, there will always be those little things, practices, and ideals tailored to different kinds of dogs. This guide will help you with all you need to know about your Maltipoo, so let's get started!

CHAPTER 2

Maltipoo History

Before we delve into the history of the Maltipoo, you should know that while the majority of dog owners call them Maltipoos, they are also called different names by different owners and even various dog clubs. The American Canine Hybrid Club and the Designer Dogs Kennel Club (DDKC) call them the "Malt-a-poo." The International Designer Canine Registry and the Designer Breed Registry use "Maltipoo." The North American Maltipoo/Maltepoo Club and Registry uses both spellings. These dogs have also even been called Multipoos and even Moodles.

However, please do not be confused; they are all the same. To eliminate confusion, we shall be referring to the dogs as "Maltipoo" in this guide.

Maltipoo Origins

The Maltipoo first appeared around 1990.

The truth is it can no longer be traced who first decided to cross a poodle with a Maltese. There are many documents and records about both the poodle and the Maltese, but not their resulting crossbreed. What can be confirmed is that these two species were first bred in the United States around 1990 after dog breeders wanted to produce a species that was small and did not shed so excessively.

However, this idea quickly caught on and before long dog breeders were breeding Maltipoos. If anyone claims to be the first to have thought of this wonderful idea, then that claim should be taken with a grain of salt.

With that said, there is also no single breeder who can claim to be the sole source of Maltipoos. So if someone tells you that you cannot get "original" Maltipoos other than from him or her, you should know this isn't true.

Different "Types" of Maltipoo

There aren't different types of Maltipoos per se, but there are different colors of Maltipoos. And for their owners, a color also serves as a type.

Before we proceed, you should be familiar with some color terms. In dog breeder or dog enthusiast parlance, a changing of the coat is called "fading" or "clearing," while the retention of a particular color throughout a dog's life is called "holding."

Black Maltipoos – Although rare, this breed does exist. A black Maltipoo will have the soft and silky hair of a Maltese, but the dark hair color of a poodle. The poodle parent will always influence the color because the Maltese is a solid-colored dog that only comes in white or cream.

For a black Maltipoo to be considered one, it has to remain black throughout its life, and not just have black hair like a puppy coat that fades to another color as it ages. The eyes and nose also have to be black as well.

You may be able to find Maltipoos with a solid black coat yet brown eyes. As is often the case, these dogs have a coat that will fade over time.

There are also Maltipoos called parti-blacks. These are dogs with predominantly black colors, meaning their coat is 50% black, and the other color or colors like blue or silver have a smaller percentage.

It should be mentioned that a true black Maltipoo can also develop a red tint in its coat if it is exposed to too much sunlight.

Blue Maltipoos – Like in other species of dogs that fall into the blue category, this shade of blue is more like a diluted shade of black.

Some are born this way, but many blue Maltipoos are also born black but fade to blue as they age. Note that it is easy to mistake a blue Maltipoo for a black one, and vice-versa.

Gray Maltipoos – These Maltipoos were either born this way from birth or had their coat fade from a rich, black color as they age.

Brown/Chocolate Maltipoos – Dogs in this category will have a color almost like that of a chocolate bar.

Just like the black Maltipoo, a true brown Maltipoo should also have all-brown eyes and nose. The same with the black Maltipoo, it is the poodle parent that influences the color.

Unlike true black Maltipoos, some brown Maltipoos may have their coat change color over time, fading to a lighter color, usually beige, even without constant exposure to sunlight. This change happens because of the dog's poodle genes.

Red Maltipoos – Maltipoo breeders consider this color the most difficult to produce. However, it should be mentioned that unlike a black or brown Maltipoo, a red Maltipoo isn't a solid red all throughout, it will be more of an apricot color with shades of a really deeper color that looks like red.

Like brown Maltipoos, some red Maltipoos will have a change of color in their coat as they grow up. So, the red areas on a red Maltipoo may fade to apricot to match the rest of the coat as the dog grows up.

Apricot Maltipoos – Maltipoos under his category are either born this way or had the red spots on their coat fade as they age.

White Maltipoos – This is usually the result when a Maltipoo is the offspring of a white Maltese and a pure white poodle. As already mentioned, pure-bred Maltese only come in white or cream; thus, a lot rides on the poodle. Breeders say the poodle has to be all-white at least five generations back before it can be bred with a white Maltese to produce white Maltipoo puppies.

Cream Maltipoos – It is easy to mistake a cream Maltipoo for a white one. According to dog breeders, any Maltipoo that is off-white is considered cream. Cream Maltipoos may also have some darker colors like apricot, gray, or tan in some regions of the body, particularly around the ears.

Café Au Lait Maltipoos – These Maltipoos will have the same shade as that famous coffee drink. The coat of this Maltipoo is described as a light and shiny tan. It will also have a liver-colored nose and dark almond eyes.

Silver Maltipoos – As in most cases, these Maltipoos are born black but will fade to shiny silver as they grow older. How can you differentiate a silver Maltipoo from a gray one? The coat of a silver Maltipoo will be lighter than a gray one and have more shine.

Silver-Beige Maltipoos – These are Maltipoos that seem to grow up beige but later develop silver hairs around the face and paws as they age.

Dog owners may have difficulty distinguishing between café au lait and silver beige Maltipoos. One thing to look out for is the color of the nose and paw pads. While a café au lait Maltipoo will have a liver-colored nose and pads, a silver beige Maltipoo will have a black nose and paw pads.

Bronze Maltipoos – This is at the bottom of the list because technically, this isn't considered an "official color" yet when it comes to Maltipoos, but that is slowly changing with more and more bronze Maltipoos coming out. Maltipoos with a lighter and shinier coat than the standard brown are considered bronze.

Nothing can stop a dog owner or dog breeder from coming up with a different color to describe a dog or when the time comes to register a dog. However, uses of words like "auburn," "liver," "vanilla," among others, add to the confusion, the colors above are the generally accepted ones when it comes to Maltipoos.

It should also be mentioned that the coat of a Maltipoo can hinge on the changing of the season. For example, some Maltipoos can have a black coat during spring and summer and a gray coat during fall and winter, then back again when the season turns.

Some Maltipoos can also change holding colors more than once. A Maltipoo may even change in the shade of its holding color more than once. They can have a particular color as they are born, but change color at eight weeks old, and then again as they reach adulthood.

Whatever the color a Maltipoo is, it will behave the same. So why do some Maltipoo owners and breeders make such a fuss about their color?

The reason for this is a Maltipoo that stays true to its holding color from birth to adulthood is considered a success when it comes to breeding. That makes them more profitable to breeders and endears them more to their owners, even though they aren't any different from "lesser" Maltipoos.

Coat

Aside from color, a Maltipoo can also have three different kinds of coats. By nature, Maltese have long straight, silky coats while poodles have curly coats that tend to cord if left to grow naturally.

Of course, this goes without saying the kind of coat a Maltipoo has will indicate if the poodle parent or the Maltese parent has the dominant gene.

Straight and silky – This means the Maltese genes are dominant. Maltipoos with straight and silky coats also tend to have a lighter color.

Thick and curly – This means the poodle genes are dominant. This coat is usually denser than the straight and silky coat.

Wiry and wavy – A Maltipoo with this coat almost doesn't feel or look like a Maltipoo at all.

Each coat has advantages and disadvantages. A long and silky coat means a Maltipoo owner can have more options when it comes to grooming the dog; it can be left long, cut short, or trimmed to something in between. However, it can also be costly to maintain.

Thick and curly hair means the dog is better insulated, and this can be a good idea when the owner and his dog live in areas where the temperature can drop. While it is less costly to maintain than a silky coat, the owner must deal with tangling and matting frequently.

Dog breeders say the wiry and wavy coat may be a sign of poor breeding and warn dog buyers to stay away from Maltipoos with this kind of coat. While this should not stop owners if they really want a Maltipoo with wiry and wavy hair, they should be aware that their coat easily tangles and can be high maintenance.

A Warning About Maltipoo Crossbreeds

Some dog breeders may have claimed to have crossbred the Maltipoo with another breed. This should be taken with a healthy dose of skepticism. You might hear about the following crossbreeds but always beware if they try to sell you any of them.

Maltipoo Chihuahua Mix – Who isn't familiar with the Chihuahua? Like the Maltese, the Chihuahua also goes way back in human history. Originating from Mexico, the Chihuahua was believed to have descended from the Techichi, a type of dog preferred by the Toltec civilization.

Chihuahuas are tiny dogs, just averaging between 5 inches (12.7cm) to 8 inches (20.32cm) tall and never weighing more than 6 lbs. (2.72 kg).

The resulting offspring of a Maltipoo Chihuahua mix isn't well established in the marketplace at the moment, and this mix may need more time to develop before it's traits can be formalized.

Yorkie Maltipoo – The Yorkshire terrier, or Yorkie for short, is another small dog that is excellent for breeding with a Maltipoo.

As per the standards of the AKC, Yorkies should stand no taller than 8 inches (20.32cm) and weigh no more than 7 lbs. (3.17kg). They have a very long coat that reaches to the ground, even when measured from their head or back.

Like the Maltese, these small dogs rooted out rodents and rats, but they didn't do this in the sun-drenched Mediterranean; they did it in the mills of Yorkshire in northern England. Eventually, they would also become the favorite of Victorian ladies because of their appearance.

Yorkies are described as affectionate, feisty, tenacious, and brave despite their size.

The Yorkiepoo cross-breed is listed with the Designer Dogs Kennel Club. The DDKC describes the dog as between 7 inches (17.78 cm) to 15 inches (38.1 cm) high, between 4 (1.81 kg) to 15 lbs. (6.80 kg), and with a full coat that requires trimming every month.

Teacup Maltipoo – There is also no such thing as a healthy "Teacup Maltipoo." If someone offers you a teacup Maltipoo, it will most likely be a poorly-bred puppy of dubious lineage. While it is true some Maltipoos may fit the size of a teacup in their early weeks, they will grow in size eventually. Spare yourself the heartbreak, and don't encourage these practices, which only harm the dogs involved.

While there are small Maltipoos, there's no such thing as a "Teacup Maltipoo" that is a healthy dog.

CHAPTER 3

The Maltipoo Breed

As earlier mentioned, the Maltipoo is not recognized as an official breed by the AKC. For dog owners and dog breeders, its classification falls under crossbreed. A crossbreed is a result when a purebred dog of one species is bred with a purebred dog of another species. A fancier term for crossbreed is "designer breed."

Maltipoo Breed Standard

As per the crossbreed description, Maltipoos can be between 8 inches (20.32 cm) to 14 inches and 2 inches (35.56 cm) tall at the shoulder and weigh from 5 lbs. (2.26 kg) to 20 lbs. (9.07 kg). Why can they sometimes get so big? This is because while some breeders seek to produce smaller dogs with a purebred Maltese and a purebred miniature or toy poodle, others breed purebred Maltese with a purebred standard poodle. A purebred standard poodle can be over 15 inches tall.

Maltipoo Breed Recognition

While this may change in the future, right now the Maltipoo is recognized only by the following bodies:

International Designer Canine Registry – The IDCR describes itself as a Christian-owned organization dedicated to facilitating the registration and pedigree services of all designer dogs.

It is run by a parent company that started registering dogs as early as 1995. The IDCR lets owners of designer dogs document the ownership, parentage, and ancestry of their dogs for whatever purpose the dog owner may have in mind, whether to sell the dog or to keep an accurate record of its lineage.

It also has several registered kennels all over the US and Canada.

The IDCR does not treat registration exclusively and is fine with letting dog owners register their dogs with both them and other kennel clubs. The founders of this registry claim a long history of over two decades in the dog breeding and training industry.

Designer Dogs Kennel Club – DDKC was established in August 2007 to cater to the needs of dog owners whose dogs aren't recognized by the more mainstream dog clubs.

Aside from providing information about health, nutrition, training, and breeding information about designer dogs, they also support adoption to move more dogs out of shelters and into homes and are active against illegal and irresponsible backyard breeders and puppy mills.

As of now, the DDKC recognizes 961 designer breeds. Aside from the Maltipoo their list of most popular designer breeds includes the Chiweenie (Chihuahua and Dachshund), Daniff (Great Dane and Mastiff), Chipoo (Chihuahua and Poodle),

Borador (Border Collie and Labrador Retriever), Chorkie (Chihuahua and Yorkshire Terrier), Pitweiler (Pitbull and Rottweiler), Labrashepherd (Labrador Retriever and German Shepherd), Newfypoo (Newfoundland and Poodle), Beabull (Beagle and Bulldog), Mastador (Mastiff and Labrador Retriever), Snorkie (Miniature Schnauzer and Yorkshire Terrier), Golden Shepherd (Golden Retriever and German Shepherd), Jack Chi (Jack Russell Terrier and Chihuahua), Morkie (Maltese and Yorkshire terrier), Borgi (Border Collie and Corgi), Boglen Terrier (Beagle and Boston Terrier), Chizer (Chihuahua and Miniature Schnauzer), Schnoodle (Miniature Schnauzer and Poodle) and more.

Just recently, the DDKC has also expanded its registry to include purebred dogs.

Designer Breed Registry – What would become the Designer Breed Registry (DBR) initially started in 1970, but did not start full operations until 1979 in Central New Jersey as The Dog Federation.

There were few members at first, but this quickly changed as more and more dog owners sought to combine the genes of different dogs and have the results registered for posterity.

In 2007 The Dog Federation transformed itself again, this time into the Designer Breed Registry.

To encourage breeders, the DBR held their own competitions, but these are not held in public. Rather, contestants submit videos of their dogs, and these are judged by a panel of three judges.

Just like other groups, the DBR also seeks to maintain a designer registry for dogs and provide a traceable lineage for the dogs of its members.

American Canine Hybrid Club – Established in 1969, this club based in Harvey, Arkansas, wants to promote more awareness of the Maltipoo breed. They do this by encouraging its members to share tips, breeding advice, and scientific studies that can help increase the success of crossbreeding dogs like Maltipoos.

Dog owners, dog breeders, and those just curious about the Maltipoo are welcome to register with them.

Like the IDCR, this club will not mind if you register with other organizations.

Aside from the Maltipoo, this club recognizes over 700 crossbreeds including the American Bandogge (Bulldog and Mastiff), Cairland Terrier (Cairn terrier and West Highland Terrier), Cavachon (Bichon Frise and Cavalier King Charles Spaniel), Cavapoo (Cavalier King Charles Spaniel and Poodle), Chi-Chi (Chihuahua and Chinese Crested Dog), Chipoo, Cogol (Cocker Spaniel and Golden Retriever), Comfort Retriever (Golden Retriever and Poodle), Eskipoo (American Eskimo Dog and Poodle), Labradoodle (Labrador Retriever and Poodle), Lha-Cocker (Cocker Spaniel and Lhasa Apso), Masti-Bull (Mastiff and Pitbull), Puggle (Pug and Beagle), Siberian Indian Dog (Siberian Husky and Native American Indian dog), Snorkie, and Yorkipoo, among others.

The North American Maltipoo/Maltepoo Club and Registry – This group aims to serve, protect, and promote the crossbreed by encouraging owners to share information about this breed. They also provide information about taking care of Maltipoos, what to expect of their temperament, breeding concerns, among others.

They can also provide information for Maltipoo breeders and buyers and the public at large.

While they encourage Maltipoo owners to register with them, they do not directly engage in finding a Maltipoo puppy for those looking to buy one. They also refuse to act as brokers in any sale involving Maltipoos. They do, however, encourage reports of Maltipoo abuse and will actively work in Maltipoo rescue and adoption. They will also work to re-home Maltipoos that need new owners.

They currently have over 58,000 members, both dog owners, and breeders, and maintain their headquarters in Grant, Alabama. Its board is currently being led by its founder, Shirley Kitelinger.

CHAPTER 4

Buying a Maltipoo

So, you have made up your mind to get a Maltipoo? Where do you get one? The good news is that there are many breeders who can provide you with one. The bad news? Some of these "breeders" may not be reliable or trustworthy. This is why it's essential to make sure you only get from a genuine breeder who knows what he or she is doing.

Choose your Maltipoo well, and you will have a playful companion for years!

Where to Get a Maltipoo?

Before we get to the part where you look for a Maltipoo, let's first talk about where you should not get a Maltipoo. It may seem like a good idea to go to your local pet store immediately. After all, why not? They might even have a "Maltipoo" already waiting for you.

The problem is that it's never apparent where some pet shops get their animals from. They can come from puppy mills or obscure backyard breeders for all you know. So you can't be sure if that Maltipoo they say they have for you is a Maltipoo at all. The pet shop may not even have enough documentation to prove the pedigree of the animal you want.

These are just some of the reasons why you should not deal with pet stores. No doubt, these are great places to get pet food and other supplies you might need to take care of your pet. However, it would be best to source your Maltipoo from elsewhere.

What about the Internet? You can buy almost everything online nowadays, why not buy your Maltipoo online? Again, this is a bad idea if you do the entire process online with no human interaction, or without getting an idea of how your new puppy has been brought up. Furthermore, you can't be sure what you will get is a genuine Maltipoo at all, and chances are unscrupulous online sellers may only be after your money and will disappear after they get it.

The best way to get a Maltipoo is to buy from a reputable breeder.

How do you find one? There are several things you can do.

Ask your veterinarian – People in this profession are likely to know who is who in the pet breeding business. This is because the people who work in these two fields share some common interests. Your veterinarian might happen to know the perfect breeder for you.

Do online research followed up by human interaction – Yes, we warned you against going online looking for puppies. However, it would help if you went online to look for breeders. A reputable breeder should at least have an established website, and preferably, allow you to speak to a few of their past clients.

Another great place to look for reliable breeders is the website of the groups mentioned in the previous chapter. Many of them have affiliated or recognized breeders.

Ask around – You should never be afraid to do this. There may be interest groups in your community that you can consult about breeders. As for online sourcing, there is no shortage of discussion boards, forums, and groups you can ask in your search for a breeder who can provide you with a Maltipoo.

One important criterion for coming up with a list of Maltipoo breeders should be how far they are from where you are. They should be within a reasonable driving distance. Surely, you don't want that dog shipped from across the country, nor do you want to drive a very long distance just to pick up a puppy.

Pick out your likely breeders and further narrow down the list. The ones who make it to the end of the selection process should be worth visiting.

If you prefer not to deal with a breeder or find their prices too steep, try looking for Maltipoos in animal shelters. Sometimes dog owners give up their pets to shelters when they are no longer able or willing to take care of them. Taking an animal home from a shelter will be good for both you and the animal. The animal will find a loving home, and you get a good pet at a fraction of the cost it will usually take to buy a new dog.

Speaking of which, how much can you expect to spend for a Maltipoo? Expect one to cost between $500 up to $2,000. A puppy from a breeder with an established reputation can also fetch from $700 to $800.

If you are offered a Maltipoo that is way below this price range, you should be wary; it may be a poorly-bred animal or a dog of dubious pedigree.

Should You Get a Puppy or an Adult?

Let's say you have already decided a Maltipoo is for you. You also already found a reputable breeder you want to buy from, the next question should be should you go for a puppy or an adult Maltipoo?

Getting a puppy means you will likely become that dog's first owner. Many dog owners think the bond is stronger between owner and pet if the owner was already there in the earliest stages of the pet's life.

However, this also means you will have to train it from the very start to do everything.

On the other hand, getting an adult dog means you no longer have to go through all that training. As an adult, it will already know how to go potty and have some obedience training. It might have even learned some tricks already.

First-time dog owners or people who have never taken care of dogs on their own before would be best served to go for adult dogs. Those who have had dogs before or taken care of dogs on their own will usually be able to take care of Maltipoo puppies.

Maltipoo Temperament

We can define temperament as the general attitude one has towards others. This can be applied to humans as well as dogs. So, what are the attitudes can you expect in a Maltipoo?

Social – Maltipoos will get along with just about anyone, whether an adult, child or another animal.

Playful – This dog is not the kind to lazily hang around the house when there is playtime to be had. Because Maltipoos are eager to please, this also makes them very easy to train.

Intelligent – Maltipoos are smarter than they look and are easy to train. They have also been found to repeat a specific behavior if they find a positive response to it.

Aside from this, a Maltipoo will always be curious about anything new. Expect your Maltipoo to go sniffing at a new dog, a new cat, or a new person they have been introduced to.

Energetic - Don't let its small size fool you, a Maltipoo is an animal that requires constant stimulation. This little dog is actually a bundle of energy, and that energy needs to be burned off. It will enjoy playtime and walking time a lot.

Loyal – Maltipoos love attention and will respond to love with loyalty. It will constantly want to be near its owner.

The Maltipoo Around Others

Given their temperament, Maltipoos are great to have around others.

Around other dogs – All dogs have a pack mentality. This instinct was from when their ancestors used to hunt, survive, and thrive in packs before they men domesticated them. Their wild counterparts still practice this in the remote regions of the world.

Give the proper introductions and allowed the adequate time to adapt or get used to them; a dog will come to regard other dogs as part of his pack.

There is no doubt that there may be some competition involved between dogs in the same living space when it comes to getting your attention or getting food. However, you should be able to get things under control as the pack leader.

Around Cats – If you already have a cat in the house and you have concerns that a Maltipoo isn't likely to get along with it or, worse, somehow end up hurting the cat, there is no need for worry.

Since Maltipoos are naturally sociable dogs, it is likely they will get along with a cat and will soon even consider it to be part of the pack. Also, because Maltipoos are mostly small, they will likely respect a cat that is around their size or bigger.

How do you introduce the cat to your Maltipoo? You do this the same way you introduce cats to each other. Start slow by letting them see each other with a door separating them. After they have started getting used to the sight of each other, have them both in the same room. They don't have to be in the same space or close together, but one room just the same. They will eventually get used to each other.

As Maltipoos are playful by nature, it might sometimes be a little too much for your cat. This is particularly the case if your cat happens to be older. Make sure your cat has places where the dog can't reach it for those times when it wants to be alone.

Around Children – A Maltipoo loves to play and will thoroughly enjoy playing with children.

There is a warning, however. Maltipoos are not recommended around very young children. Children under six years old may not yet be able to discern between playing with the dog and putting it at risk.

Many Maltipoos have suffered fractures after little children picked them up but dropped after they could not hold on to them. Rough play from children can also injure a Maltipoo.

If there is no way you can't have one without the other, make sure you are always there to supervise when they are playing together.

With single people/families – It doesn't matter if you are a person living alone or if you have a huge family. As already mentioned, the dog's pack mentality will kick in. And the dog's concept of a pack also extends to humans. That pack can be as small as is just you and the dog, but it can also be as big as you and the dog plus several others.

It will come to consider you and the humans it associates with you as part of its pack. It will come to trust and love people it realizes belong to the pack.

Pros and Cons of a Maltipoo

We all know that everything in life has advantages and disadvantages. What are the pros and cons of owning a Maltipoo?

Cons

They are small and could get injured more easily as a result. They were bred to be that way. This puts them at a disadvantage when dealing with something bigger, like a child, a cat, or a bigger dog. They may also be easy to miss when they go under a vehicle, furniture, or someone carrying a box or bags of groceries.

They aren't suited to be guard dogs (if that's what you are looking for) – If you got the Maltipoo thinking it can add a layer of protection around your home, then you thought wrong. The Maltipoo was bred to be a companion dog, not a guard dog.

Although it may have the instinct to protect its owner from danger, as all dogs do, you can't expect it to do much. The best, or worst, a Maltipoo can do is nip at the ankles of one threatening the owner.

They are a relatively new breed – Because Maltipoos aren't recognized as an official breed by major canine organizations, it tends to leave them left out where recognition is concerned. That is slowly changing, however.

Pros

They will always look like puppies – Sometimes, dog owners wish their dogs would stay puppies forever. While a Maltipoo will mature in intelligence as it grows older, it can still look like a puppy for the rest of its adult life.

They are ideal for small places – Since they are small dogs, they don't require much when it comes to space. This makes them suitable for single apartments, tiny homes, and other similar spaces.

They also don't require a big space or backyard to run around in, unlike the bigger dogs. As for exercise, a walk around the block will do for this little dog.

They don't shed – Since they were bred to be hypoallergenic dogs, they won't shed as other dogs do. This means you won't have much of a mess to clean up around the house. Also, you don't have to worry about hair getting on your clothes when you handle them.

They adjust well to new environments - As long as you are with it, a Maltipoo can handle being taken outside your house, or to a completely new environment like another neighborhood or even another house.

They are smart – As mentioned earlier, they are easy to train and will tend to repeat something to which their owner acknowledges positively.

They don't cost much to feed – Their small size means they won't require much food as bigger dogs do.

Is it Easy to Care for?

This is perhaps the biggest question on the mind of anyone who wants to get a Maltipoo. The truth is that the Maltipoo is just as easy to care for as any other dog. It will require love, attention, care, and the occasional trip to the vet. Also, Maltipoo owners also have to remember the following.

They will crave attention – A Maltipoo will seek you out for company and will always want to be near you. This may become an issue for people who don't like animals that are too clingy or don't have the concept of personal space.

Don't leave them alone for long periods of time – A Maltipoo should be able to tolerate being alone for a few hours while you are at work or away. However, if you happen to be away for a big part of the day, then you should consider adjusting your hours, make sure the dog has company while you aren't there, or get another kind of dog entirely.

You shouldn't leave them outside for extended periods – Maltipoos weren't bred to be outside dogs. The occasional walk around the neighborhood is ideal and good for the dog, no problem with that. You should also let the dog outside to do the call of nature. However, they should not be left out for long periods of time. Due to its small size, a Maltipoo is already vulnerable to dogs, strangers, cats, and even birds of prey. Leaving them outside increases their vulnerability.

They will require daily care – In particular, Maltipoo pups have to be brushed daily to keep their hair from getting matted and tangled. They also have to be bathed every three weeks or so.

They will become a product of their environment – If you live in a tense household where there is a lot of animosity and shouting between the family members or residents, then the dog might become a shy and withdrawn creature. It may soon avoid spending time with you and the others.

What you have to remember here is that like raising other kinds of dogs, a Maltipoo will require commitment. Spending time playing, exercising, grooming, and taking care of a Maltipoo will take up time that can otherwise be spent doing other things.

You may find less time for other things if you get this kind of dog. So if you can't commit to taking care of a Maltipoo, then you shouldn't get one at all.

However, what is certain is that if you dedicate enough time and care to your Maltipoo, it will provide you endless hours of entertainment and affection. You will soon find that all the time you devoted to taking care of your dog will be worth the time lost doing other things.

CHAPTER 5

Your Maltipoo Puppy

It is the first three months of a Maltipoo puppy's life that are the most important. It's during this brief window of time when the puppy's temperament, behavior, and character traits develop.

This is why you have to be a positive influence during those three months. The things you do, whether they are right or wrong, will impact how your Maltipoo will behave for the rest of its life.

Be sure you know how to pick the right Maltipoo puppy!

Maltipoo stages

Before we get further into its early development, a Maltipoo owner should learn more about the stages in a Maltipoo's life.

From birth until six weeks, they are considered newborns; they should not be separated from the mother, and it must be ensured that they can get constant nourishment from her.

From eight weeks old, they are officially considered puppies and are can now be adopted into new homes.

The period between the third and fourth months can be considered their "teething period." This period will also be, as mentioned earlier, their equivalent of the human "formative years."

Between four to seven months old, they are already considered as entering dog puberty. The females will start to get in heat, and the males will already begin producing sperm.

At one-year-old, they officially become young adults. They become full-blown adults at three years, and seniors after their eighth year.

Now that you realize you have a limited time to influence your Maltipoo, you shouldn't waste any time at all.

Picking the Right Breeder

Before you get to choose the puppy, you must decide which breeder to choose. In the previous chapter, we cited distance may be a significant factor in selecting a breeder. This is so you can drive there and back, hopefully with a puppy in tow.

Even if a breeder is recommended by your vet or that community you consulted online or in person, you should still watch out for the signs that they may only be after the money, or aren't really outstanding breeders.

Avoid buying from them if:

- They keep marketing the small size of the Maltipoo as a selling point
- They produce too many litters in a year
- They don't show any concern for the animals

- They don't want to make any guarantees. A good breeder should offer to take the dog back for any justifiable reasons

Another thing to look out for is a waiting list. A good breeder might already have a lot of people waiting to buy.

When faced with a litter of Maltipoos, you might be tempted to immediately choose the one you find cutest then go on your way. But before you even pick one, you must talk to the breeder about several issues:

Ask about the puppy's parents – Find out if the puppy's parents are certified and ask to see them.

Ask about their health – Have they been dewormed? Have any puppies in the litter been sick? What vaccines of the puppies received?

Ask about their temperament – You will be in charge of molding their behavior later on, but this early it always pays to ask if they a puppy has been socialized or not, how it acts around other pups, among others.

The answers to these questions should help you finally decide if you want a puppy from this breeder or not.

How to Choose the Right Puppy?

A puppy should be ready for a new home between eight to nine weeks old. However, the longer you wait, the better the puppy will get. An eight-week-old puppy tends to be less adventurous and assertive as a 10-week-old puppy.

A healthy puppy should be alert, lively, and curious about the world around it. Ask to see it walk; it should not wobble as it moves.

It should feel firm in your hands, not limp. Its eyes should be clear, and there should be no discharge from its eyes, mouth, nose, or anus.

While dogs can have a particular odor, a healthy puppy should not smell bad.

What Color to Go for?

This is entirely up to you. Remember that some colors are rarer than others and that in some Maltipoo puppies, the colors tend to fade as they age.

Ask the breeder about the pedigree of the puppies. The breeder should know what lines tend to fade or hold their color.

If you are wondering whether to go for a male or female, there isn't much difference. However, it has been observed that the females tend to be more independent and the males more outgoing. Females are also slightly more trainable than males as they easily get distracted.

It appears she has chosen well!

Bringing a Puppy Home

Preparing to take the puppy home should begin long before you get the puppy. You don't want to get a puppy, only to realize you don't have the things you need to transport it safely.

Aside from the vehicle, you will be using, you will need a kennel crate, a dog plushie, a pee pad, and a towel.

The kennel crate is for safely transporting the dog. You don't want it running free in your car as you drive home.

The plushie is to be used for an old dog owner's trick. After you are sure that you have picked the right dog and payment has been made, bring the plushie to the littermates of that puppy and make sure they get their scent on the plushie. If your puppy is the last of the litter to be sold, the scent of the mother should be sought.

Have the plushie with the dog in the crate as you drive home. The smell on the plushie will remind the new puppy of its first family and keep it calm. It is even advisable to keep the plushie around until the puppy feels it no longer needs it.

The pee pad is for any accidents along the way; the towel is to keep the dog warm on the drive home. Make sure the kennel is securely strapped in before you drive.

Puppy-proofing the Home

Preparing your home for a puppy should also be done before you go to get the puppy. You don't want to drive home with a puppy, frantically calling on the phone for anyone at home to quickly make it dog-proof or dog-friendly.

Puppy-proofing your house doesn't mean a huge renovation. It just means making certain parts of the house safe for its latest inhabitant.

You might be tempted to corral the puppy in a small area and keep it there for a few days. However, because of its nature, it will want to explore its new surroundings. Getting to know its new environment is also ideal for any dog in a new place.

There is another reason why you should do secure your house; puppies explore with their mouths. They don't have any hands to hold or examine things, and the mouth is the only tool they have at this stage. They also like to knock things over, crawl into tiny spaces to see where they go, as well as pull or push on things.

Here are the areas around the house you should secure:

Stairs – Sometimes, dogs can go up the stairs but can't make their way down. Then they hurl themselves down and take a tumble. Secure your stairs with baby gates top and bottom. You may go through the hassle of opening and closing them as you use the stairs, but it will be worthwhile to keep the puppy safe.

Kitchen – There are sharp tools in the kitchen that may pose a danger to your puppy. There may also be a trash bin that can present an aroma of new smells for a curious dog.

Bathroom – Like the kitchen, the bathroom can contain items with chemicals that can be harmful to a dog like soap, shampoo, conditioner, and shaving cream. There are also discarded tissues, Q-tips, cotton buds, and other items that can arouse a curious dog's sense of smell.

Bedroom – There are many things that a dog may like to chew on in your bedroom. Like your slippers, clothes, hair ties, and other items. Your pillow or blanket can also become fair game if it's within their reach. Keep these items off the floor.

Garage – There may be dangerous chemicals within easy reach of a Maltipoo puppy in your garage. There may also screws, nuts, nails, and tools like hammers, screwdrivers, or wrenches precariously perched on benches and worktables. Make sure your puppy cannot reach them.

Yard – This can seem like a very harmless place; after all, it's where many dogs play. However, a yard can contain plants that can make a dog sick or kill it. Make sure you know what houseplants and outside plants have toxic effects on dogs. The yard might also have a shed that has items like pesticide, fertilizer, and rat poison.

Other areas in the house – Keep electrical cords where the puppy cannot chew them. Unplug items which aren't in use, and make sure the cord isn't within easy access of the puppy. Make sure there are no little objects on the floor like buttons, paper clips, and the like. Puppies are notorious for swallowing whatever gets them curious enough.

The golden rule when it comes to securing your house is to consider what your puppy might be able to reach. Anything that it can potentially get its mouth should be stowed away or kept out of range.

This is not to say you should allow your puppy into all the rooms of your house when he arrives; it is just to make sure he is safe if he somehow finds its way to those areas.

Puppy Spaces

Before you get the puppy, you should also already assign places where it should sleep, eat, and where it should go potty.

Position the pee pad near the door to the outside (this will be explained below). Place the eating area where people don't frequently pass; this will be to keep the puppy safe. And set a special place for the dog's soft bed.

You should set a space just for the puppy in the house before bedtime. It is advisable to set up baby gates to corral an area where you set up the dog bed. This is its special area for now and your puppy can't go outside the gates at night. You don't want it wandering around at night unsupervised while everyone is asleep. These can be removed as the puppy gets more and more comfortable with the surroundings.

Choose a spot where there is no draft so the puppy can be comfortable. At this point, it is also advisable to position this puppy space somewhere; it can hear your voice without necessarily seeing you.

The First Few Days

After arriving in your home, your family members might be all gathered and waiting to greet and hold your Maltipoo puppy. It isn't advisable to welcome it this way. This might prove too much for the puppy as it is still adjusting to a new environment.

The first thing you should do is take the puppy to where it should go potty in your backyard. That should be the first place it remembers. Try to wait until it does its business before taking it inside.

Introduce the puppy to your family, but don't let them hold it and pass it around. Let the puppy sniff their hands and get acquainted with their scent.

Let it wander around the house but under your supervision. It will also help if you encourage it to follow you around. Talk to it often, get it used to the sound of your voice.

Keep the dog plushie in the soft bed. That way, the puppy will feel assured when it sleeps.

The first night is usually the roughest for a puppy. It will howl, whine, and cry out for its mother and littermates. If this goes on for some time, call out to the puppy every once in a while; it will want to hear your voice.

Over the next few days, take the dog on walks to become familiar with the neighborhood. Before you leave your yard, make sure it pees where you took it the first time it arrived. After you come back from the walk, wait until it pees there again.

Family training – It's not just the puppy who will go through something new. Your family will also have to adjust to having a new member of the family.

Many people think it's a good idea to keep puppies a surprise until they arrive. While the intention behind this is good, it may be a bad idea in the long run. Telling your family about what to expect and how to prepare for the puppy will go a long way to making sure nothing bad will happen.

Make sure they understand that the dog will be a small one, so little, in fact, it can get in their blind spots if they are carrying something and easily trip over them. It's so small that it can get seriously hurt if caught in the door, or accidentally kicked.

They should also be told that the dog is not a toy and shouldn't be handled like one. It must be held tenderly and supported throughout the entire length of its body.

You must also show them the proper way to hold a Maltipoo puppy, one hand around the dog's chest to keep it from jumping and the other hand under the dog to keep it from slipping under.

They should also be advised to help keep the house puppy proof. Ask them to pick up little objects on the floor, close doors to rooms the puppy shouldn't enter, and make sure nothing dangerous is within its reach.

Family members should also be advised to exercise patience with the newest addition to the family.

Pet Training

As soon as your puppy has adjusted to its new surroundings and new family, you should begin training. At this stage, the most important thing you should do is teach it to do its business outside.

Potty training – We mentioned earlier that you should place the pee pad near the door to the outside. The more the puppy uses the pee pad, the more it will associate peeing with the door; this will make it easier to get him to associate the door with "doing business."

Make sure to praise them when they use the pad. You can eventually take the pad outside behind the door; the puppy will not be able to see it but can smell it. It will indicate that it wants to go outside. Again, praise it when it uses the pad. Finally, you can position the pad near where you brought the puppy to pee the first time. The more it gets familiar with the yard, the more it will go outside to use that particular spot for its business.

Biting training – Another thing to teach your puppy is not to chew on the wrong things. As mentioned, the puppy's third to fourth month is its teething phase, and it will bite and chew on anything it can get their mouth on, including your hand.

Discourage biting by flicking the end of the puppy's nose, coupled with a stern "NO!" Soon, he will associate that reaction with negative behavior.

If you see him chewing on something he shouldn't be, repeat the reprimand firmly but calmly, then quickly replace that object with a chew toy. Praise the puppy when it starts chewing on the chew toy; he will remember this positive acknowledgment and learn.

CHAPTER 6

Your Pet Maltipoo

Some types of pets require more attention than others. Pets like cats have their share of care needed; however, they usually like to be left on their own. Pets like goldfish only require regular feeding and a clean tank, but they aren't mobile and will not always seek to get your attention.

Before You Get One

The same cannot be said for the Maltipoo. This pet will continuously try and get your attention and affection. So unless you are prepared to give attention whenever it's asked for, or at least most of the time, you will have a hard time adjusting to a Maltipoo.

The Maltipoo's diet changes as it grows.

Feeding Your Maltipoo

The first thing you have to remember is that your Maltipoo will need different amounts of food at various stages of its life.

Before you implement any feeding regimen, it will still be best to consult your veterinarian. The puppy might be more similar to either the Poodle ancestry or the Maltese ancestry, and the veterinarian might be able to identify some issues that come with this.

However, the rule of thumb when it comes to feeding Maltipoos is that a Maltipoo puppy will require more food as it grows from being a puppy into an adult. And, adults will require less food than a growing puppy.

Give the puppy an ounce of food per day for every pound that dog weighs. Let's say you have a Maltipoo puppy that weighs five lbs., you should give it five ounces of food per day. When it reaches six lbs., add another ounce to its daily diet, and so on.

After your Maltipoo has reached adulthood, that is one-year-old, you can now cut down to giving it half an ounce of food per day, for every pound it weighs.

Another thing you need to remember is that Maltipoos are tiny dogs. As a result, it is easy to overfeed them. While this may not have any immediate negative impact, it will be detrimental to the Maltipoo's health later on when they become overweight. This can lead to other complications like diabetes and heart failure.

What to Feed Your Maltipoo

As a growing animal, your Maltipoo puppy must get the following:

Carbohydrates – To provide energy.

Protein – To build muscles and body tissue.

Fats and fatty acids – To maintain healthy skin and promote cell growth.

Vitamins and Minerals – To boost the dog's immune system, balance chemicals in the dog's body, and maintain its muscles and bones.

Check the labels of dog foods for those ingredients.

On the other hand, there are things that you should **avoid** giving your dog. If you happen to see any of these ingredients in dog food, avoid it at all costs.

Meat byproducts – This can actually be any part of any animal. Sometimes animals that are considered too sick for human consumption are ground up and made into these, so you need to be careful here.

However, there are exceptions. If a product label specifies the meat byproduct is made from human-grade organ meats like liver, heart, and kidney, it should be safe for your dog.

BHA or BHT – Butyrate Hydroxyanisole and Butyrate Hydroxytoluene, are both harmful preservatives.

Corn or corn syrup – The former can develop fungus or mold and make your dog sick. The latter can cause a condition in your dog that is similar to diabetes in humans.

Soy – This is good for female humans but bad for dogs because of the damage they cause to their endocrine system.

Some people prefer to feed their dog human food or scraps from the table. However, this isn't ideal because it will only teach the dog how to beg and may result in them overeating. Feeding them your scraps also isn't a guarantee they will be getting the nutrients they need.

Homemade Dog Food

There is also the option to make your own homemade dog food. The recipe many owners recommend is a mix of protein (50%), cooked vegetables (25%), and starch (25%).

You can source protein from meat products like pork, chicken, beef, lamb, and even fish. It would also help to throw in organ meats like liver, heart, or kidney.

Make sure you finely chop vegetables. Dogs' teeth are designed to tear up meat, not grind up plants. Doing this will help them process it more efficiently. Another thing you have to make sure of is that the vegetables are well cooked; dog's stomachs are not designed to break down plants as well as herbivore stomachs.

As for the starch, you can get it from brown or white rice. If your dog is observed to be intolerant to gluten, you can substitute with gluten-free pasta.

Both commercial dog food and homemade dog food have their advantages and disadvantages.

Commercial dog food doesn't need any preparation on your part, aside from serving it to your dog. It can also save you the time needed to prepare the food. You can also be sure many of the nutrients good for your dog are already there.

On the flip side, commercial dog food has many ingredients that you can't separate from the food. You can also not be sure they have quality meat byproducts. Sometimes not all dog food put all the ingredients in their nutrition label.

On the other hand, with homemade dog food, you can be sure of the quality of the ingredients you put in. You can also be sure you aren't putting in anything your dog might be adverse or allergic to. It also may be cheaper in the long run, compared to commercial dog food.

As for its cons, homemade dog food can take time to make. It also has a limited shelf life. You can also be never sure of the exact amount of nutrients your dog is getting with homemade dog food.

A Good Balance

While homemade dog food can be used when the commercial dog food isn't available, it's not meant to replace it entirely. The best practice is to supplement your homemade dog food with a portion of high-quality commercial dog food.

It is also advisable to switch between commercial dog food and your own homemade dog food every once in a while. Believe it or not, dogs also experience the boredom that humans go through when eating the same thing every day.

If you plan to wean your Maltipoo off one or the other, do so in stages. If you are using commercial dog food and plan to have your dog get used to homemade dog food, start by putting a little of it in your dog's meals every day. After they have gotten used to it, you can gradually increase the amount over time, adding more and more, and using commercial dog food less and less until you stop using it altogether.

If you want to wean your Maltipoo off homemade dog food, you can use the same process; gradually add increasing portions of commercial dog food into their meals.

How Often to Feed Your Maltipoo

For puppies, it is ideal for them to have several small meals a day. Remember how much they must eat and give food according to the puppy's weight. Divide the daily amount it should get by the number of meals. If a puppy is five lbs. then you should give it five small meals, at one ounce of food each.

After the dog has reached nine months old, you can feed it four times a day, still according to its weight. When the dog reaches adulthood, you can now limit the feedings to twice a day, and at the recommended amount of half an ounce of food for every pound it weighs.

The ideal time to feed the dog is in the morning and at night. Preferably it should be after you have breakfast and dinner; that way, you can set a schedule that you and the dog can get used to.

It's essential to set a scheduled eating time and not just feed the dog when you remember to, or feeding it if it asks for food. Having more control over its feeding habits means you will have more control over its food intake and its health.

Your Maltipoo's Living Environment

We have already discussed how to make the area puppy proof, but creating a living environment for your Maltipoo is a different thing. Don't get the wrong idea; you shouldn't go to the extreme of tailoring or renovating your house to make it livable up to dog standards. You are the owner of the property and also of the pet. The house should be according to your living standards as a human being.

Creating a living environment for a Maltipoo only means that you make sure you have everything a Maltipoo needs when it comes to not just living in your house, but also what they need to be a happy, healthy pet.

Maltipoo Living Space

Because it's a small dog, Maltipoos don't require too much space. However, they must have the following:

An indoor living space – If you bought a Maltipoo with the intention of letting it sleep outside the house, then you are making a big mistake. Maltipoos aren't outside dogs.

This isn't to say a Maltipoo can never be allowed outside. They should go out when it comes time for walks or to go potty. However, you cannot expect them to stay outside for the long term, exposed to the elements, and at risk of being attacked by dogs and other animals.

Their small size can also make it easier for them to slip under gates or fences.

Access to water – Food is something you should give your dog at regular and set intervals. However, water is something it should have access to whenever it wants. All that running around can cause a dog to be dehydrated.

There are dog bowls that can hold food on one side and water on the other; this is a good idea to save on space. However, if you prefer to have a separate bowl for dog food, the ideal place for a water bowl is the same area where the food bowl is located.

Constant company – Maltipoos were bred to be companion dogs, so after they have formed a bond with you, they are likely to always look for your company. If you have to be away for a good part of the day, think about having an additional pet so that it won't get restless and unhappy.

Access to potty options – Sooner or later, a dog will have to do its business, as humans do. If you have trained your dog enough, it should know better than to go potty in the house and make indications that it wants to go outside for this purpose. However, you also have the option to train it how to use a litter box.

While you may be familiar with litter boxes for cats, there are also litter boxes for dogs. And the Maltipoo happens to be ideal for the use of litter boxes, because of its size.

Place the litter box in an area that isn't frequented by the rest of the family.

If you happen to have a cat, make sure the dog has its own litter box. Animals should not share a common litter box.

Access to the outside – While Maltipoos should be indoor dogs, it is also good to let them outside every once in a while to run around the yard.

Other Ideal Conditions

So, you have provided your dog with a place to sleep. Sometimes this might not be enough. Make sure the space is well ventilated but not susceptible to drafts or moisture. It should also not be too hot or too cold.

It should also be a place quiet enough for the dog to rest, so setting the dog bed beside the washing machine or other things that make loud, continuous noises isn't a good idea.

You should also buy toys for your dog. They like to be stimulated by different things like chew toys, puzzles and interactive toys, and the like.

Maltipoo Socialization

Since Maltipoos can get along well with other dogs, it can handle another dog in the house, or go on walks where it can meet and socialize with other dogs. Dog socialization is crucial for your Maltipoo; it builds their confidence in dealing with other dogs as well as other humans.

A dog that is kept sheltered in a house will likely become shy and withdrawn when it comes into contact with other dogs and humans aside from its owner.

If you see a familiar dog, encourage your Maltipoo to socialize with it. This will go a long way toward building its character.

CHAPTER 7

Caring For Your Maltipoo

Your Maltipoo will have needs that go beyond just food, water, and shelter. As a companion animal, it will also need a lot of love and affection from you.

The good news is there are many ways you can ensure this.

Playing and Bonding

There are several ways you can show your dog you love it.

Petting – For a dog, a petting will feel like a gentle massage. Petting can calm down an uneasy or nervous dog.

The thing is that dogs don't like to be touched on the top of their head, which is a pity because many people like to pet dogs beginning with touching the top of their head. They will not show any resistance if you do this, however. But many don't like it.

The right way to pet a Maltipoo begins with a light touch to the back of the neck. From there, you move in long, slow strokes in the direction the fur goes, not against it. You can also do light scratches instead of long, slow strokes.

Rubbing their ears – This might seem cliché, but a dog loves it when you rub their ears. This is because, in canines, there is a high concentration of nerve endings around their ears, making it very sensitive to the touch. So when you rub their ears, and they look like they are enjoying it, they actually are.

Feeding them by hand – Putting food into a bowl for your dog to eat is one thing, but feeding it by hand is entirely another. It's a trust exercise the goes both ways; the dog has to trust you that you are giving it something safe, and you have to trust the dog that it won't bite you.

If you are concerned about getting bitten, you shouldn't worry. The muscles on a dog's jaws allow them to exert the slightest force possible, and they can also tell when they are clamping down too hard on anything and relieve pressure immediately.

Belly rubs – Belly rubs also feel good for dogs because stimulating the hairs in that area sends signals of pleasures to the brain.

When your dog approaches you and exposes its belly, it's actually a sign that a dog trusts you and submits to you. This behavior comes from their ancient ancestors. To show submission, a dog will expose its belly – hence its vital organs - to the pack leader.

Other touches – Maltipoos like to be caressed in the base of the neck, the shoulders, and their chest. Some also like to be touched under the chin and the back part where their body meets the tail.

Telling them you love them – Dogs are smart, and they can seemingly understand some words or at least the feeling behind the tone associated with these. This is proven by their recognition of their names and their response to obedience training. Tell them you love them will reassure them that you have a special place in your life.

Make sure the tone of your voice matches the message. It would be best if you didn't scold a dog in the same tone of voice you use to express affection or praise.

A Maltipoo at play – energetic when excited!

Maltipoo Exercise

You might think that because a Maltipoo is a small dog, it doesn't need exercise. However, like humans, they also need it.

Dogs get the same benefits we do when it comes to exercise. It builds muscles, improves the blood flow, promotes a healthy heart, and keeps the weight down. Regular exercise will also lead to a healthy appetite and regular sleeping patterns.

In dogs, regular exercise will also burn off any extra energy. This is energy that might be spent chewing on anything it shouldn't be chewing around the house.

A dog that stays indoors will not get as much exercise as a yard dog. This is why you should encourage your Maltipoo to play outside every once in a while.

Considering it is such a small animal, playing around a yard for 30 minutes is enough. If the weather happens to be particularly hot like in the summer or cold like in the winter, you can cut down the time to half.

If you live in a part of the country that sees snowfall, be sure you are there to watch over your dog.

Maltipoos love to go for walks.

Walking

Playing around the yard should never take the place of walking. Aside from being the best form of exercise for your dog, it's also an experience for your pet; it gets to deal with different kinds of terrain, it gets to see and smell different things, and may also even meet other dogs along the way.

Make sure you and your dog are ready to deal with the outdoors.

Leash and harness – Some cities have laws against dogs if out in public places without a leash. Getting the right leash and harness for your Maltipoo will be discussed later in this chapter.

Collar – Your dog should have a collar stating its name, your name, and your address. Your contact details can also help, although many dog owners prefer just to put their address.

Why do we recommend a leash and harness combination instead of a leash and collar? A harness is better when it comes to exerting control over your dog when it is out in public. When you attach a leash to a collar, you are putting it at risk because the collar wraps around the dog's neck. There is always a risk of suffocation if the leash is pulled too high. You can also damage the dog's trachea if you suddenly yank the leash.

When you pull on a harness, the pressure will not be concentrated on the dog's neck. It will be distributed throughout its chest, back, and shoulders. A harness will also make it easier to pick up the dog in case the need arises.

Water bottle – This will be for the water for both you and the dog.

Collapsible bowl – Pour water into this container to let your dog drink. Many pet shops now carry various models of this kind of container.

Tissue and plastic baggie – This is for when your dog might have an accident out in the street. It is good dog owner courtesy to clean up after your pet. You most likely want other pet owners to observe the same courtesy, after all.

Cleaning up after your dog is also a good way to prevent diseases from spreading among animals in a neighborhood.

Dog treats – Why bring dog treats during a walk? So you can reward it for any good behavior it shows. Who says training begins and ends in the house?

Two 20-minute walks per day should be enough for a Maltipoo.

During hot weather or anything above 85 degrees Fahrenheit, make sure your dog is equipped to deal with the environment. You may not be able to feel the hot pavement because of your shoes, but for your dog, it will be like its walking on hot coals. Have your dog wear dog booties or apply pad wax to their feet before you set off.

Consider a shorter walk if the temperature happens to be high. This will also cut the risk of your dog getting heat exhaustion or a heat stroke.

You can also try walking early or late in the day to avoid the worst of the heat altogether.

If the weather happens to be cold or snowy, you should put a dog jacket on your Maltipoo. Dog clothes aren't just for show; they can keep your dog warm too.

You should also pay attention when walking your dog in snowy conditions. Some cities treat certain parts of the sidewalk with chemicals to melt the ice. These chemicals can be harmful to your Maltipoo's feet.

Exercise isn't limited to yard play and walking; playing fetch with your dog or hide-and-seek around the house can also count as exercise. And, so does any cardio activity done for a period of time.

Maltipoos can be trained to manage being alone well.

Maltipoo Separation Anxiety

The first time you brought home your puppy was its first experience with separation anxiety. It likely cried and whimpered all night, or at least most of the night, because it missed its littermates.

You eventually became the family it no longer had, and you even became the pack leader.

However, one day, you just suddenly up and left. You might just be out for work or groceries. But the dog doesn't know that. It also doesn't know if you will be back.

When your Maltipoo realizes that it is alone and that it cannot find you no matter where it looks, it will start to get stressed and anxious. It will again experience separation anxiety.

If the dog's unease goes on for a prolonged period, your dog will start to channel that worry into activities, kind of like the way we humans do when we want to distract ourselves from thinking about something too much.

Unfortunately for humans, those activities are destructive, dirty, or downright disgusting.

Chewing spree – A dog suffering from separation anxiety can start chewing on things. And this can be anything it can reach or come across like books, furniture, throw pillows, the carpet, and even your shoes.

Scratching around – A dog distressed will likely scratch at any door, thinking it might find you behind it. The more is scratches, the likely it will destroy doors or injure itself.

Incessant barking and whining – Barking and whining is one way for dogs to get attention, and it will do this if you are gone because it thinks it will get your attention and bring you back to it.

Pacing – Just like a worried human, a dog left alone will be pacing to and fro with apprehension.

Going pee and potty – Dogs usually do this to mark their territory. However, exactly why dogs do this when under anxiety has not been fully explained. They just do it. Needless to say, it will be very messy for you when you come home.

Excessive panting – The dog going pee and potty isn't actually the worst thing that can happen. Sometimes they can practically feel so much distress they begin panting excessively. This has even led to heart failure.

Do not mistake these things, especially the destructive behavior, for acts of vengeance your dog is carrying out for leaving you alone. They did these things because there was no other way for them to express their worry and agitation.

How do you deal with separation anxiety? It all goes back to the first night the puppy spends at your house.

Remember that we suggested to let the puppy spend the night alone. Within hearing distance of your voice, but alone, nonetheless. This is to teach it to learn to be by itself for short periods.

You can reinforce this behavior in two ways; by rewarding good behavior like being quiet and settled down, and by deepening your dog's trust in you.

You can begin teaching your dog to get used to time alone by having it lie on the floor. You then hide from view but come back. Discourage it from looking for you. After it has understood what behavior you want from it, increase the time you are out of sight. Don't make a grand exit when you go or grand entrance when you come back. Make sure the dog gets the idea it will become a routine event that you will occasionally disappear but always reappear.

Building trust will further enforce the dog's belief that you will always be back no matter how long you are gone. There are several things you can do to strengthen the trust between you and the dog.

Act like the pack leader – This doesn't mean you order the dog around all the time and continuously boss it. This means you maintain a calm demeanor that the dog will interpret as confidence. As mentioned in a previous chapter, a house with a lot of shouting and tension will have adverse effects on a dog. In your case, if you show behavior where you are almost always upset or agitated, the dog will get the impression you are not in control.

Minimize noise – Dogs are very sensitive to loud sounds and will interpret big noises as danger. If they are constantly living in what they perceive to be a threatening environment, then they won't have much trust in you.

So even if you are angry, don't slam the door. If you are enjoying music or a movie, don't turn the volume way up. If you are upset at someone, do your utmost not to raise your voice. If you are excited, minimize the screaming. Even the hum from electronic devices that we can't hear can be painful for dogs, so turn them off when not in use.

Show by example – When you see your dog do something it isn't supposed to, your first instinct might be to spank it. The problem is that the dog won't understand why it's being spanked. It will only realize, that for a brief moment, you suddenly caused it pain and that you might be able to do so again.

For example, if you see your dog biting something it shouldn't, don't resort to spanking. As mentioned in a previous chapter, say "no," accompanied by a flick of the nose, then direct them to what they should be chewing, in this case, a chew toy.

If you catch them in the act of peeing, say "no," accompanied by a flick of the nose, and take them to the dog litter box.

Be the dog's pal – Even as you are the pack leader, you can still be a "friend" to the dog. Be the one that comforts it when it is scared, the one who opens the door when they need to go potty, the one who fills up the water bowl.

Doing little things like these, among others, will reinforce the dog's belief that you are someone it can rely on and someone who has its interests at heart.

The more your dog trusts you, and the better it is trained to spend time alone, the easier it will be to leave the dog alone for longer periods.

As a last resort, you can resort to giving your dog a companion toy. This is a toy that looks like another animal that can give your dog the illusion that it isn't alone until you get back.

Maltipoo Transport

Sometimes you have to take the Maltipoo out of the house and even out of the neighborhood. Maybe it's time to take it to the vet, or the dog park because playing in the yard and walks have become boring. Whatever the reason, you will need the standard leash and harness plus a choice of several devices.

Maltipoo leash and harness – We already covered the purpose of the leash and harness earlier in this chapter. How do you pick the right one for your Maltipoo?

When it comes to leashes, you can choose between two kinds. A retractable leash will let you maintain control over your dog even as it allows your dog to explore a little further. A standard four- or six-foot leash with a loop can also be used on your dog.

As for the harness, pick one that fits your dog's size. In this case, small. Make sure you choose one that allows for adjustment. When you put a harness on a dog, make sure it isn't too tight. Allow space for a finger's breadth between your dog's body and the straps on a harness to give it a little leeway.

Maltipoo dog crate - A 19-inch kennel crate will suffice for the average Maltipoo, but there are also larger models for slightly larger Maltipoos.

If you use the crate mainly to transport your Maltipoo to the vet, it will eventually come to associate the crate with something terrible, especially if your dog doesn't like the trips to the doctor.

How do you train a dog not to be afraid of the crate? One thing you can do is get your Maltipoo used to the sight of the crate. Don't just take it out when you want to use it. Leave it somewhere around the house where the dog can see it, and it will soon associate it with everyday objects.

Another thing you can do is encourage your dog to stay in the crate. You can encourage your dog to go into the crate by offering treats or by putting its bed there.

When transporting a Maltipoo using a crate, make sure it is already in the crate before you take it to the car. Securely fasten the crate before driving off.

Dog car seat – These are small boxes that you can secure to the front passenger seat or the back seat. Your Maltipoo can rest snugly inside it.

Dog car harness – This is a special harness that allows you to clip your dog to the seatbelt of the backseat. It's a smaller version of a five-point harness that race car drivers wear.

Dog car seatbelt – This is a strap that has a clip on one end and a seatbelt tongue on the other. The clip fastens on to the dog's harness, and the tongue can be inserted into the seatbelt buckle.

Each one has its advantages and disadvantages. A kennel crate allows your dog more freedom of movement, but it can be heavy to put into the car with the dog inside already.

A dog car seat will give more freedom to your dog, but it can't offer much protection in case of a collision.

A dog car harness can offer the best protection for your dog in case of a collision; however, this also prevents any kind of mobility since its paws will be up in the air.

A dog seatbelt provides the best mobility for the dog, but also leaves it vulnerable to the stop and go motions of the car.

It's up to you what product to choose, but it would be best to have more than one and pick the right device for the right occasion. The longer the drive, the more important it is for your dog to be able to relax.

Your Maltipoo probably won't mind being practically immobilized in a dog car harness for a short drive. However, it might start to get antsy if it's strapped in one for a long ride. A dog seat belt isn't the best idea for a trip with a lot of traffic where your car stops and starts often. A dog car seat may be appropriate if you just had certain medical procedures done on the dog, and so on.

Other Things to Remember

Make sure your Maltipoo is secured – Before you drive off, make sure the dog is strapped in, buckled in, or securely fastened in whatever device it is using. You don't want to start moving, then suddenly notice the dog is running around in the vehicle.

Be sure it is comfy – If you are using a dog car harness and it is restrained too tightly, your Maltipoo might start to whine to get your attention. If unattended, it might even lose blood circulation.

Another thing you can do to keep the dog relaxed throughout the trip is to make sure you maintain a calm environment. Don't shout at other drivers, lay off the horn as much as possible, and don't play the radio music too loud.

You can also bring along its favorite toy to keep it occupied.

Make regular stops – People on long drives often stop to stretch their legs and breathe the outside air. Your dog will also need this if the trip happens to be a long one. Just be sure you keep an eye out for it by leashing your Maltipoo before you release it from the device; it might just run out of the car in its excitement.

Another reason you have to do this is that some dogs suffer from motion sickness. However, if they still keep suffering this despite frequent stops, your veterinarian can recommend some medication to ease their suffering.

Always carry water – As if you are going for a walk, always have that container of water and the dog's collapsible bowl.

Use window shades – Like humans, dogs can be bothered by too much or direct sunlight. Use shades to protect your Maltipoo.

Maltipoo Toys

Over the course of its life, a Maltipoo will need certain toys to train it or to keep it occupied. There are four general categories of toys for dogs:

Teething toys – Dogs chew because they experience discomfort as their teeth develop. These toys are good for them, and also are meant to replace the other things in your house the dog might end up chewing instead.

Interactive toys and treat-dispensing toys – These are toys that help develop a dog's intelligence. Some of these are toys that give dog treats when they figure out how to solve a problem. Some make attractive sounds when activated.

Playtime toys – These are toys you can play with your dog. These come in the form of balls, items that can be used for fetch.

Companion toys – As mentioned earlier, you can have several toys that look like other animals for your dog to play with.

Except maybe for the companion toy, a toy should never take your place as its owner and best teacher. Remember that toys are there to help you take care of the dog, not to take your place.

CHAPTER 8

Grooming and Bathing Your Maltipoo

The Maltipoo isn't a breed recognized by the major kennel organizations, so it can't be considered a show dog. However, it's still one of the cutest dogs around and has to maintain its looks to stay that way. Grooming and bathing also have a practical purpose; a well-groomed dog will be happier and less susceptible to diseases, illnesses, and other health issues.

Keeping Your Maltipoo Clean

It would help if you started grooming your Maltipoo as soon as you get it. Don't begin to groom them only after they have become adults, or it will become more difficult for them to sit still and behave them during your grooming sessions, or worse, at bath time.

Maltipoo "Shedding"

Maltipoos were bred to be hypoallergenic dogs, so they don't shed. However, this doesn't mean they stay neat all the time. While they don't shed hair, they still shed dander, which can cause allergies in some humans.

Over time a Maltipoo's coat can also get tangled and matted. It will become more and more uncomfortable for your dog. This is another reason why it's important to bathe and groom them.

Grooming should begin immediately as soon as you get a puppy, but not bathing. As soon as it is born, it's the puppy's mother who assumes the role of cleaning the puppy. This role passes on to you as its owner.

However, it's not advisable to start traditionally bathing your Maltipoo, until it is 8 weeks old. This is because, up until this age, puppies are still developing the natural oils that keep their skin moisturized. During this time, they are also still unable to regulate their body temperature, and as a result, they can feel chilly easily.

"Bathe" puppies at this age by wiping it with a damp cloth.

After your puppy has reached eight weeks, it should be ready for its first traditional bath.

Maltipoo Bathing

Be sure you are ready for the bath before you give it; otherwise, it will become quite the experience for you and your Maltipoo.

1. Prepare the things you need - Before you even start the bath, have the things you need ready. You don't want to have a wet dog on the loose while you rush around to grab the things you should have prepared in the first place.

Shampoo and conditioner – Be sure to choose the kind of shampoo that's good for the type of hair your Maltipoo has.

Cotton balls or cotton gauze – Stuff these into the ear of the dog to prevent shampoo or water from entering.

Mineral oil – This protects dogs with sensitive eyes against the shampoo.

Towels – To dry the dog off, and yourself too if things get too exciting.

Treats – These will help the dog associate bath time with treat time, and they won't think about bath time negatively.

Note that treats can also be used to keep dogs calm or distracted during a bath. Some companies sell pads that can be stuck to the wall. You can apply a spread of peanut butter or anything the dog likes, to the pad. Bathe the dog while it is happily eating the treat.

Brush – Give your dog a quick brushing after the bath.

Large basin – You will only need this to rinse your dog off if you don't have a flexible shower hose.

It's ideal to bathe your dog in the bathroom tub or sink. Never do this in the kitchen sink, even if you have a flexible hose there. You don't want a wet dog running all over the kitchen. You also don't want dog hair down the kitchen drain.

2. Prepare yourself – While the Maltipoo isn't a big dog, its splashing might still get you wet, so you better dress in clothes you don't mind getting wet in. Keep in mind that you are going to get hairy and dirty, so wear clothes appropriate for this occasion.

3. Prepare your Maltipoo – Before bathing it, make sure its nails have been trimmed to prevent any injuries to either of you.

Bring your Maltipoo into the bathroom and shut the door to prevent escape. Give the dog treats and talk to it to help make it feel comfortable. Stuff the cotton into the dog's ears gently.

4. Fill up the sink or tub with warm water – Do this before you put the dog in. Many dog owners make the mistake of putting the dog in the sink or the bathtub before they fill it up. Then the animal gets excited, thrashes about, and makes a mess wetter than it ought to be.

Another mistake is putting the dog in when the water is still too hot, as this may scald the dog and give it a bad impression about bath time.

5. Begin the bath – Put the dog in as soon as you are sure the temperature is right. Begin by wetting the dog's coat with water. Leave the head for last to keep it calm. After it is wet all over, start applying shampoo at the shoulders then move on from there. Take care when applying shampoo on the head; this is where they are likely to get uneasy. Be careful when using shampoo around the eyes, nose, mouth, and ears.

As you rinse the dog, use your fingers to feel if all the shampoo has been washed away.

Follow up the shampoo with conditioner. As many conditioners require some time to pass before rinsing off, use this time to clean the dog's ears with the cotton balls stuffed inside them. Replace them with new ones for the rest of the bath.

6. End the bath – Rinse off the conditioner. Again, use your fingers to make sure no trace of it is left on your Maltipoo.

7. Dry it off – After the bath is done, immediately take out the dog from the sink or tub, then dry it off with a towel. Dogs usually shake themselves off after a bath, but this isn't enough to totally dry it off, so you have to help.

Brush your Maltipoo; this will get rid of any loose hair.

Don't forget to take out the cotton balls out of its ears.

Remember also to dry the dog's feet thoroughly. It will be running around the house when you let it out from the bathroom, and you don't want wet pawprints all over the house!

Take the effort to make the first bath as nice and uneventful as possible, and your Maltipoo should have no trouble cooperating in future baths.

Giving your Maltipoo a bath every three weeks is ideal. Remember that Maltipoos aren't outside dogs, so they shouldn't get that much dirt on them. They are also the kind that doesn't shed, so three weeks between baths should be sufficient. If you give them more frequent baths, you risk drying their skin because you are washing out their natural oils.

A Maltipoos coat needs to be maintained.

Maltipoo Grooming

Going to a professional groomer to get this done is always an option. However, why not do the grooming yourself? Grooming is one of the things that you can do that will deepen the bond between you and your dog even more. And you can save the money otherwise spent on professional grooming.

How you groom your Maltipoo depends on what kind of hair they have.

Straight and silky hair – If they have this kind of hair, the good news is that this type of coat isn't prone to tangling. You can have a Maltipoo with this kind of hair groomed every six to eight weeks.

Thick and curly hair – This kind of coat will be prone to tangling and matting. It will need regular trimming to keep it from growing out of control. The recommended time between grooming is four weeks.

Wavy and wiry – This is a lot like thick and curly hair, but even harder to keep clean. Dog owners with a Maltipoo of this type of hair tend to keep the coat short to save them the trouble. Like thick, and curly hair, the recommended time between grooming is also four weeks.

As earlier mentioned, begin grooming your puppy as soon as you get it. Before its first grooming session, show it the brush. Get the puppy used to its feel, appearance, and smell.

After it has become familiar with the brush, start brushing the dog lightly for about a minute. Indicate that you want it to sit still while it is being brushed. Praise the dog, then give it a treat for doing so.

Do the same thing over the next few days to establish a routine with the brush. Never use the brush to spank the dog, or threaten it.

For the grooming to be a pleasant experience, you both have to be in the right mindset. If you happen to be upset and start grooming your dog, your mood might affect how you stroke your dog, and it will have an adverse effect. In this case, wait until your mood improves before you groom the dog.

If your dog happens to be the one fidgety during grooming, you can either use more positive reinforcement like treats or encouragement. You can also keep the grooming session shorter.

As with bathing, take the effort to make your first grooming session as routine and uneventful as possible. If the dog finds its first experience with grooming unpleasant, it will likely be uneasy during future grooming sessions. Or it may even try to avoid one altogether.

Professional Grooming

While you may be able to do an excellent job grooming your dog, it really wouldn't hurt to bring it for a trim from expert hands every once in a while. A groomer will also be able to give your dog a professional haircut that you may not be able to replicate.

Maltipoo Care Supplies

There are many brands for dog shampoo and conditioner, so how do you choose the right one?

Be sure you know what your dog needs. Early on, it's advisable if you get a shampoo that is specifically formulated for a puppy's developing coat. But as it ages, it may have to need a different kind of shampoo depending on its skin type, whether it has normal, dry, or oily skin.

Let's say your dog develops dry skin as it grows older, go for shampoos that have ingredients like vitamin E and aloe.

Another thing you have to consider is its coat. If your Maltipoo has a coat with long hair, it's best to choose a shampoo that will create a rich lather, so that it can reach the roots of the hair.

Dogs with a particular odor can use a deodorizing organic shampoo.

If your Maltipoo regularly comes into contact with ticks and fleas, get a shampoo that is specially formulated to deal with these pests.

Choose the right pH level - Dogs have more sensitive skin than humans, so they need a shampoo that falls within the 2.2 to 7.5 pH range.

Choose a shampoo your dog isn't allergic to – While the dog may not be allergic to a particular brand itself, it may be allergic to one or some of the ingredients in the shampoo.

How can you tell if your dog will have an adverse reaction to a particular shampoo? You can do a "patch test" where you can test the shampoo on a small area of your dog's coat. If that one spot doesn't do well, don't use that shampoo.

Read reviews/ask other dog owners – Look for comments from other pet owners about specific products. If you have some doubts about reviews, ask other dog owners about their experiences with certain products. You can also ask about what they recommend.

Another person you can ask is your veterinarian. Since their business involves treating animals, they should be familiar with certain shampoos that are good for certain types of dogs.

Maltipoos need baths too!

Don't Use Your Shampoo on Your Dog

Shampoo formulated for human hair isn't ideal for dog hair. Dog shampoo will be different when it comes to thickness and consistency, among other things, because dogs are different from humans when it comes to hair, skin, pH level, and even the glands in their skin.

Using your shampoo on a dog will not only have no beneficial effects for your dog, but it could also cause the dog's sky to dry and flake off.

CHAPTER 9

How to Train Your Maltipoo

Performing tricks is one of the ways dogs entertain their owners. There is a sense of achievement in watching a dog do something that has taken a long time to practice.

However, training your Maltipoo isn't just about teaching it tricks. A dog should be able to recognize its name. It should be able to identify and obey specific commands like "sit," "stay," and "come."

With more training, you should also be to train it to stay off particular furniture, stop jumping on people, and also keep off the bed.

How Difficult are Maltipoos to Train?

Like its parents, Maltipoos are easy to train and will respond to positive reinforcement. Don't use negative reinforcement like spanking, as this will only confuse the dog.

They should be trained as soon as they arrive in your house; while it has been proven that old dogs can learn new tricks, it is easier to train them while they are young.

Equipment You Will Need

Treats are the necessary reward for training. These treats should be different from the kibble you feed your dog, so they will come to regard it as special. There are different bite-sized dog treats available in the market today.

Alternate between different treats to allow for variety. Half a dog treat should suffice like a small dog such as a Maltipoo; if you are concerned that it will be eating too much.

What to Train Your Maltipoo

How to recognize its name - The first training a Maltipoo needs is to know its name. That way, it can tell when you are addressing it directly or calling it to you.

As puppies are easily distracted. Make sure you take the puppy to a place where there aren't things or sounds that can take your puppy's attention away from you.

Call it by its name in a high-pitched and happy tone. This is to have the puppy associate you are calling its name with a positive mood. Remember that puppies can sense emotion even at a young age.

The behavior you want to see in the Maltipoo is to have it look at you and establish eye contact with you when it hears its name. Whenever it successfully does this after you call out its name, praise it. While you might be tempted to reward it with a treat each time, hold back on this. It will make the treat seem even more special. Offering a treat for doing the behavior you want three times in a row should be appropriate.

However, it would help if you didn't hold back on the praise. Whenever your dog does the behavior you wanted it to do, praise it in the right tone. Make sure it understands you are happy with its behavior.

For the next stage of this training, move to an area of the house with a little more noise and distraction, then repeat the training until you get the results you want.

Keep doing this until you get to the room in your house with the most noise and distractions and train it there as well until it learns its name.

Obedience training – In dogs, obedience training means being able to recognize and respond correctly to commands like "sit," "stay," and "come." These are particularly useful when you want a dog to follow you, stop following you, or keep away from specific areas.

Maltipoos are very intelligent and can be taught to obey commands.

Teaching Your Dog How to Sit

Take the dog to the room in your home with the least distractions. Stand facing the puppy and dangle a treat in front of its nose. Let the puppy nibble on the treat before slowly raising the treat. This will force the dog to raise its head and shoulders slowly, and drop its hindquarters. When it reaches that position, say the word "sit." Praise the dog and give it another treat. Repeat the training.

If the dog doesn't drop its hindquarters while reaching for the treat, you can assist by touching its back and coaxing its behind down, while saying the word "sit." Be as gentle as you can if you have to do this.

As with the previous training, keep repeating the process in areas with more and more noises and distractions until the behavior you want is established.

Teaching Your Maltipoo to Stay

The "stay" command will come in handy as you train your Maltipoo to spend time alone by itself to prevent separation anxiety.

To begin training, have the Maltipoo assume the "sit" command position. Put your open palm out in front of its face and say, "stay." The behavior you want from it is to do nothing for a few seconds. If it moves or responds to the command differently, have it "sit" again and then repeat the new command with the accompanying hand gesture.

If you get the behavior you want, praise the dog. If it keeps repeating unwanted behavior, keep resetting it back to the "sit" position, don't offer praise or treats, but you shouldn't show frustration either.

Once your dog finally displays the behavior you want, back up a few more steps and repeat the process until it is reinforced. As with the previous training, repeat the process in rooms with increasing noise and distraction until the behavior is learned.

You should also lengthen the time you require the dog to stay. Work up the time until you can achieve the goal of having it stay still a few minutes. Also, work on your distance from the dog. With enough training, you can eventually train it to sit and stay in that position even if you aren't in the same room.

Teaching Your Maltipoo How to Come To You

Once your Maltipoo has mastered how to "sit" and "stay," then "come" should be the natural follow-up.

Have your dog assume the "stay" position until it reaches the time you want. Then say the command "come" in an enthusiastic voice while holding out a treat. It should obey the command willingly and eagerly. After it does, give it praise and make sure it understands you are pleased with its behavior.

It's ideal to restart the dog to the "stay" position immediately after it has learned the behavior you want from it.

If it acts too early and rushes to you without your command, say "no," and reset it to the "stay" position. Don't give it a treat or any praise.

As with previous training, repeat this process in areas with increasing noise and distraction. Work until such time that the dog will be able to respond to your command even as you are out sight but within hearing.

You can also teach your Maltipoo to lay as flat as possible with the "down" command. Do this by bringing a treat to the floor with your hand and encouraging the dog to follow. Gently push it down as you say the word "down," then reward it with a treat.

Keep repeating until you no longer have to physically push it down anymore and it responds correctly to the command.

Teaching Your Dog How Not to Bark

Take note that, like other dogs, Maltipoos bark as a form of communication. They will bark for four general reasons:

They are afraid – Perhaps they see something that's out of place or smell something that raises their alarm.

They are lonely or bored – A dog that is frustrated because it is lonely or bored can let off steam by barking.

They see a threat – If they see an animal or human that is not familiar to them, they will start barking

They want your attention – If they're going to call your attention to something, they will bark. They might want you to fill up the dog bowl, let them out for playtime, potty or pee time, among others.

What you should not do is shout at your dog to stop barking. If you do this, it will only get more excited, thinking you are joining in on the barking and make even more noise.

If your dog starts barking, the first thing you should do is ignore it until it stops. After it has stopped, tell it "hush" or "be quiet." Wait half a minute, then praise it and give it a treat.

As with other commands, you can repeat this process until it has learned the proper response to this command.

Another thing you can do is distract or interrupt your dog. When it starts to bark, call it over and distract its attention on something. The more you do this when they are barking, the less they are inclined to bark.

Teaching Your Dog How Not to Jump at You

Your puppy may jump at you when it sees you because it is happy, but when it starts doing this to any guests who enter your home, it may soon become embarrassing.

The best way to discourage this behavior is not to show any excitement when the dog greets you this way. Greet it calmly, if it sees you react when it jumps on you it will think it's doing the right thing and keep on repeating this behavior.

You can also ignore the puppy if it jumps on you, only acknowledging it after it has calmed down.

If your puppy keeps on jumping on you even if you have greeted it calmly or even gone to the extent of ignoring it until it calms down, you can say the word "off," then accompany it with the gesture of walking away and ignoring it. Only approach it again after it has calmed down, then give it praise.

To keep your guests from being jumped by the puppy, ask them to do as you did. Ask them to ignore the puppy until it has calmed down. When the puppy is no longer excited, you may now allow your guest to approach and greet it.

How to keep your Maltipoo from jumping on the bed or other furniture – If you happen to be on the bed or the sofa, then your Maltipoo is likely to want to join you there for a cuddle. Some owners like this behavior, but others don't.

If your Maltipoo keeps getting on the bed or sofa with you, give it a stern "no," accompanied by you gently removing the animal from the bed or couch. Place it on the floor where you want it to be while you are on the bed or couch.

If it persists with trying to climb on, leave the room, and ignore the dog. Keep doing this until it understands you don't want it to do what it's doing.

Maltipoo Tricks

These are a step above the basics. You can teach your dog these tricks the same way you train it to obey the simple commands; with treats, trial and error, repetition, and a lot of patience. Note that you can teach your dog a lot more tricks than these, but these are the most famous.

Shake – Teach your dog to hold it its paw when you hold out your hand and say, "shake." Tell it to assume the "sit" position then indicate what you want it to do. It may help if you physically move its paw into your hand as you say the command word. Keep repeating until the dog understands what you want it to do, then reward with treats and praise.

Roll over – Have the dog assume the "down" position, then hold a treat against its nose. Move your hand from the nose to the shoulder to make the dog lie on its side. Reward and praise the dog once it has learned to do this.

During the next session, move the treat past the dog's shoulder to its backbone, which should force it to lie flat on its back. Reward and praise it again.

For the next session, continue moving the hand with the treat until the dog completely rolls over. When it does, say the words "roll over." Keep repeating until it correctly responds to the command.

Fetch – You need to be really patient with this, the thing is that there are dogs that retrieve what you throw, but don't take it back to you, keeping it for themselves instead.

Start with choosing the right toy to get your dog's interest and attention. Get your dog used to it. Tease the dog by grabbing the toy and tugging on it, as if you want to get it. Be very gentle when doing this, and make it enjoyable to the dog. Take the toy entirely, then tease the dog further by wiggling the toy a bit, then toss it a short distance away. If the puppy does nothing, entice it by wiggling the toy on the ground.

Once your puppy takes the bait, engage it with another game of tug. Take the toy again and repeat the process. Reward its reaction with another fun game of tug.

Your Maltipoo will soon understand that you will reward it with a game of tug if it takes the toy to you. During the next session, put the toy at your feet and step back a bit, encouraging the dog to take the toy and approach you for a game of tug.

Gradually increase the distance you put between you and the toy, making sure the dog does what you want it to do. You can even start running away, so your dog will have to chase you. As usual, reward the expected behavior with treats and praise.

Over time you should be able to throw an item and have the dog take it and bring it back to you without you having to move from your spot.

Training Yourself

Over the long run, you will find out that it won't be just you training your Maltipoo, but you will also be training yourself as well as the process goes on.

Remember that as a trainer, you have to display certain "behavior" as well:

Be patient – Your Maltipoo will not be able to understand what you want from it immediately. This is not unlike a person learning a new skill.

Be consistent – If the dog displays the behavior you want, respond accordingly with praise and the occasional treat. Make sure this reaction is consistent when it does what you want it to do. On the other hand, if the dog doesn't do what you want it to do, reset it to the starting position, and repeat the process.

Timing is everything – Remember that you have to let a dog "do the wrong thing" before you praise it for doing the right thing. Like waiting for it to stop barking before getting it used to the "hush" or "be quiet" command. Or waiting for it to assume the right position to teach it the "sit" command. Recognize the right time to teach your dog what you want from it.

Don't show your disappointment – If your dog does the opposite of what you want it to do, don't make disapproving sounds or show your frustration. Above all, do not punish it physically with a kick, knee, or elbow; this will only confuse the dog.

Keep training sessions short – Like humans, dogs will also get tired after "school," so keeping training sessions to 5-10 minutes each to maintain their interest and cooperation.

CHAPTER 10
Maltipoo Health

It's your responsibility as a dog owner to make sure your Maltipoo is healthy. A healthy dog is a happy dog. And a happy dog can make its owner smile even more.

Signs of a Healthy Maltipoo

There is a "checklist" you can go through every day to make sure all is well with your Maltipoo:

Eyes – These must be clear without any trace of discharge. The whites of the eyes shouldn't be tinted with yellow or bloodshot.

Ears – There should be no blockage like ear wax. There should also be no unpleasant smell.

Nose – A nose on a healthy dog must either be cool and moist, or warm and dry. There must be no discharge. If there is a green discharge, that might mean your dog has a bacterial or fungal infection.

Mouth – No bad breath or warts. The cause of warts will be explained further in this chapter.

Breathing – Rasping or wheezing breath could be a sign of illness.

Behavior - Your dog should also be quick to be up and about, if it seems lethargic or unwilling to engage, it might have health issues.

A healthy Maltipoo is a happy Maltipoo!

When to Be Concerned

Now that you know the signs of a healthy Maltipoo, you should also know the signs when it could be in trouble where its health is concerned.

High temperature – Dogs should be warm to the touch. However, if they feel overly warm, like the way a human feels when one has a fever, this should be taken as a sign that something is wrong. By four weeks or older, your dog should have a temperature of between 99.5F and 102.5F.

Difficulty breathing – See if your dog has difficulty breathing or experiences shortness of breath.

Change in temperament – If your normally-loving Maltipoo may seem suddenly irritable or quick to anger, then there is something wrong.

Limping – Your dog is doing its best to avoid using one leg or another. Or it may even not be able to stand up at all.

Excessive drooling – Dogs usually drool at the sight of food, but if your Maltipoo is drooling more than normal, take it as an indication of something wrong.

Loss of appetite – Dogs love to eat, so if your dog suddenly loses its love for food, then something is wrong.

Seizures – Dogs can suffer from epileptic seizures; this will be discussed in further detail later in this chapter.

Uncoordinated movement – Your Maltipoo may seem like it cannot control its muscles, no matter how hard it tries.

Vomiting and diarrhea – The same with humans, this is always a sign your dog needs medical attention. Dry heaving or retching should also be taken seriously.

Urinary problems – If your Maltipoo has difficulty peeing, or cannot pee at all, this is an indication it needs help.

Abdominal pain – If your dog has a swollen abdomen or experiences abdominal pain.

If you see any of those symptoms in your Maltipoo, it may be a good idea to contact your veterinarian. Those might be indications of illnesses and maladies that we will discuss later in this chapter.

Maltipoo Lifespan

The average lifespan of a Maltipoo is 12 years. However, if you happen to take exceptionally good care of your Maltipoo, it might even live up to 14 to 16 years old.

The lifespan of this crossbreed is influenced by the parents of the dog. The Poodle and the Maltese can each live up to 12 to 15 years old.

Maltipoo Food Allergies

While there are foods you should give your dog, there are also other foods that you should never give to your dog. At least not in excess. Take note that these foods may be used as ingredients in some of the foods you intend to feed to your Maltipoo.

Make sure the rest of your family, the other humans in your house, or those you might recruit to watch over your Maltipoo, know what is harmful to your dog.

Cooked bones – Yes, bones are suitable for a dog because they do wonders for their teeth and give them nutrients the body needs. However, they have to be raw bones. Cooked bones tend to splinter in your dog, causing possible damage to the windpipe, esophagus, and internal organs.

You also have to be mindful of the size of the bones since Maltipoos are small dogs. Pick a big bone that the dog can gnaw on, but not swallow.

Chocolate or coffee – These two have the same effect on a dog; ingesting a little can cause them to have upset stomach and diarrhea. A lot will wreak havoc on their circulatory system and cause heart failure, ultimately killing your dog.

Certain fruits – Some fruits can actually be good for your dog, but not all. Avocadoes have a toxin that also upsets the balance of the dog's digestive and circulatory system, causing an upset stomach and even heart failure.

Pear seeds contain a sufficient amount of arsenic that can be fatal to a Maltipoo. Peach pits turn into cyanide into a dog's stomach. Fruits like plums and persimmons can also become a choking hazard for such a small dog. Raisins can cause damage to their organs like the liver and kidney.

Sugar and sugar substitutes – A little sugar won't harm your Maltipoo, but if it eats too much of it, it can become obese, and this can lead to complications.

Sugar substitutes pose a more direct threat to dogs. Substances like Xylitol can cause them to go into a seizure and die.

Certain spices – Spices like garlic, leeks, chives, and onions can cause anemia at best. In the worst-case scenario, they can wreak havoc on your dog's circulatory system, ultimately causing heart failure.

Cinnamon – When inhaled, cinnamon can disrupt a dog's respiratory system. When consumed, it does even worse and causes upset stomach, vomiting, and liver disease.

Nuts – Almonds can damage a dog's windpipe and esophagus. Nuts like pecans, walnuts, and especially macadamias are poisonous to your Maltipoo.

Salt – Salt increases water retention. It can also ruin their circulatory system and ultimately lead to heart failure.

Liver – Like sugar, a little of it now and then is good for your Maltipoo, but if they have too much of it, this can be bad for their muscles and bones.

Alcohol – A little can cause the same effect in humans; lack of coordination and intoxication. A lot can cause your dog to go into a coma and die.

How might your Maltipoo ingest alcohol, you may ask? They might lick it from discarded cans in the kitchen, so be careful where you throw those away.

Maltipoo Immunizations

Vaccination is a must for your Maltipoo. This is to protect them from viruses from any source, including other dogs, and also to protect you as the owner. You should also vaccinate your dog if you plan to frequently take your Maltipoo to a dog day-care or kennel, or to a park to socialize with other dogs.

At five weeks, the main concern should be parvovirus. Puppies happen to be at high risk of this. Canine parvovirus can be transmitted from one dog to another by direct contact or indirectly through their feces. This is why it's essential as a dog owner to always clean up after your dog in public places.

The mortality rate in puppies with parvovirus can be as high as 90%.

Between six to eight weeks, give your Maltipoo what is called the combined vaccine, also known as the Five-way vaccine. It is meant to immunize your dog against adenovirus cough, hepatitis, parainfluenza, and also parvovirus.

At 12 weeks your Maltipoo is ready to be vaccinated for rabies. The law varies in different states as to what age to have your dog vaccinated. But for Maltipoos, this age is ideal.

At 15 weeks, it's advisable to take your Maltipoo to the veterinarian for another combined vaccine. This vaccine should deal with leptospirosis, Lyme disease, and coronavirus.

When it's over a year old, and already an adult dog, give it another booster shot of the previous vaccine.

If you are worried about not being able to keep track of what your dog needs, there's no need to fret. Your veterinarian should provide you with a booklet to keep track of what vaccinations your dog has or hasn't received.

Medical Conditions and Their Solutions

There are several maladies known to affect Maltipoos. Because they are considered a crossbreed, and breeding has never been a precise science, the Maltipoo can become prone to some of these medical conditions and birth defects. Here are some of them:

White Shaker Syndrome – This may be noticed in puppies as young as six months old and up to one to two years of age. You might notice them suddenly having tremors all over their body, or exhibiting rapid eye movement, and lack of muscle coordination, especially when it becomes stressed or excited.

While it might be disconcerting for you to notice this condition, the good news is your dog isn't in any pain. It will also not affect your dog's personality in any way.

However, you should still ask your veterinarian about how to deal with this condition. Treatment with corticosteroids may be recommended.

Epilepsy – Similar to a human having a seizure, your Maltipoo will start to shake uncontrollably for a few seconds, sometimes even longer.

While the episode will not kill your Maltipoo, it can still die as a result of their temperature getting too high. This usually happens if the seizure goes on for more than five minutes.

Like in humans, medicines can be used to effectively treat, but not totally cure, episodes like these.

Patellar luxation – This is a birth defect that doesn't manifest in your Maltipoo until it grows old. If you notice it starting to limp with a skipping or hopping motion, it can be a result of patellar luxation.

This happens when the patella - made up of the thigh bone, kneecap, and calf - are not aligned properly as a result of the birth defect. The result is that the bones rub on each other because they aren't aligned properly, and this can make the Maltipoo's leg limp.

There are degrees of severity, called grades, for patellar luxation. In Grade 1, the symptoms will be mild and infrequent; in Grade 4, lameness and limb deformation will be observable. At this stage, a surgical procedure might be required.

Portosystemic shunt – If you notice your puppy suffering from lack of appetite, stomach issues, and an overall lack of balance when it is around two years of age, this might be a result of having a portosystemic shunt.

This happens when the blood flow between the dog's liver and the rest of its body becomes abnormal. Like in a human, the dog's liver is also responsible for detoxifying the body and metabolizing the nutrients from the food it eats.

This condition can also be confirmed if the above symptoms come with hypoglycemia and stunted growth.

A special diet consisting of little to no meat, breakfast cereal, vegetables, and even fruits safe for dogs can correct this condition, but it may also require surgery in severe cases.

Legg Calve Perthes Disease – This is a disease that is common in small dogs. If your Maltipoo has this condition, the head of the femur bone on the dog's hind leg will start to degenerate. This will result in the slow destruction of the hip joint and also cause bone and joint inflammation.

The immediate cause remains unknown, but veterinarians think this is caused by the loss of blood flow to the head of the femur bone.

This usually happens in puppies around four to six months old. The usual symptom is limping. You may also notice its leg muscles have become stiff. The usual solution to severe cases is surgery.

Retinal Atrophy – This is a genetic disease that affects certain breeds of dogs. Similar to what is called retinitis pigmentosa in humans, pigments in the dog's eye slowly build up.

The peripheral vision of the do will go first, then total blindness will follow. It can take years for a dog to become totally blind.

Sadly, there is no treatment for this disease. The good news is that if your Maltipoo ever gets the misfortune of having this illness, it can still live a happy life using only the rest of its senses.

Canine oral papilloma – These are warts that can build around the lips, gums, and mouth of a dog. This usually happens before they reach two years of age because, at this age, their immune systems haven't fully developed yet.

Warts are caused by a virus that can be transmitted from one dog to another by direct contact, drinking from the same bowl, using the same chew toy, or sharing the same food bowl.

Over time these warts can cause pain, bad breath, and swelling. By itself, warts should disappear between one to five months, depending on your dog's immune system, but you shouldn't take the chance.

Antibiotics ought to cure mild cases of this illness. However, in more severe cases where warts have become infected, there has to be surgery.

Colitis – This is an inflammation in the large intestine of the dog. It can be caused by many things, including bacteria like salmonella, E. coli, giardia, and even stress.

If your Maltipoo seems to experience pain while pooping and the feces have small amounts of bright red blood, this is often an indication of colitis. The feces will also appear to be semi-formed or totally liquid.

Your veterinarian should be able to recommend a diet to treat this.

We aren't saying your dog will suffer from any or all of these illnesses within its lifetime. However, it pays to be prepared and know what you and the dog are facing if they do occur.

Pros and Cons of Neutering / Spaying

It's always advisable to have your Maltipoo spayed (for females), or neutered (for males), unless you will be showing the dog or breeding them.

Before you think this is inhumane, consider that the Maltipoo is already a crossbreed, it's likely a first-generation Maltipoo. If you breed it with another Maltipoo, the result is what is called a second-generation Maltipoo.

Second generation Maltipoos will not have the same qualities as a first-generation Maltipoos. They will also be prone to more health issues than their first-generation parents; this is why many Maltipoo owners decide to have their pets undergo this neutering procedure.

Spaying is done by sterilizing female dogs, to make sure she no longer enters her regular heat cycles. The procedure involves making a small incision in the dog's abdomen and removing the uterus.

Doing so will make a female Maltipoo less nervous, and lessen its chances of barking or crying. There will also be no chances of unwanted pregnancies.

The ideal time for female Maltipoos to undergo this procedure is between four months and six months old. However, this can also be done on older dogs with no side effects.

Neutering is done by removing the male dog's testicles, leaving only the scrotal sac behind.

This procedure will make the male Maltipoo less aggressive, less likely to mark their territory by peeing, and less competitive with other animals or people in the house.

Unlike female Maltipoos, which can still undergo their procedure even after six months, it is advised that male Maltipoos get their procedure done before they reach six months of age. This is because, by six months, they have already built up testosterone in their body, causing them to act as if they were not altered.

Male Maltipoos neutered over six months of age also have the tendency to become obese as they grow older.

The only cons of spaying or neutering your Maltipoo is that it will no longer be able to reproduce, which, as stated earlier, is not a good idea, and also it will cost you money. Also, most showing standards dictate they must be intact if that is a consideration for you.

How to Choose a Good Veterinarian For Your Maltipoo

We have previously mentioned you need to always ask your veterinarian about your Maltipoo's health issues. However, we have never talked about the veterinarian itself.

How do you make sure you choose the right one? You might be tempted to go for one that doesn't charge a lot. However, as the saying goes, you usually get what you pay for. A cheap veterinarian can also mean he or she isn't fully accredited to handle specific procedures, or qualified enough to make certain diagnoses.

Just like when you first searched for a breeder, find the ones closest to you, then make a list of them. It won't do you good if you seem to find the perfect veterinarian for you but is located too far away to be a practical choice.

From there you should narrow it down after the following:

Make sure he/she has AAHA approval – The American Animal Hospital Association sets the standard for animal clinics. While it's true that a lot of good clinics don't have AAHA accreditation, going to a clinic with one will ensure you get a certain standard of service.

Get recommendations – This is where other dog owners can help. Ask the ones who meet in the dog park, or even your neighbors, if there is a vet they can recommend.

See the office – A well-equipped clinic should have the necessary equipment needed to diagnose and treat what ails a dog like X-ray, ultrasound, IV pumps, and the like. It should also be able to do basic laboratory tests, so you don't have to go to another clinic or a dog hospital.

Talk to the staff – Are the staff familiar with how to take care of animals? Are they passionate about them? Or are they just in it for the paycheck?

Availability – Last, but not the least, make sure that your veterinarian can be available at all hours in case of emergencies.

Choosing the right veterinarian for your dog can mean the difference between a healthy dog and a sickly one. It can also be a matter of life and death for your Maltipoo.

CHAPTER 11

Maltipoo Breeding

There are those who breed Maltipoos for a living. Their livelihood, as well as their reputation, depend on what they do, so it's understandable they will want to keep certain trade secrets to themselves. However, we can offer some advice for those who want to breed a Maltese and a Poodle on their own to produce their very own Maltipoo.

Some terms must be defined before we proceed. The word that breeders use for the female parent in a pairing is called a dam, while the male parent is called a sire. It doesn't matter what breed the dog is. The female is always called the dam, and the male is called the sire.

Getting a dam and a sire to mate is called a tie.

The offspring of such a pairing is called a first-generation Maltipoo. The offspring of a pairing between two Maltipoos is called a second-generation Maltipoo.

To produce a Maltipoo, only a purebred Maltese and a purebred Poodle should be used. They can't have a mix of anything else, or the resulting offspring may not have the characteristics of a Maltipoo.

Because there is no standard size for a Maltipoo, it may seem confusing at first.

How to Breed the Best Maltipoo Possible

It's understandable you want to have the best Maltipoo that can result from a pairing. This is why it is also advisable to have both parents tested for eyesight problem issues, hearing loss issues, and possible hip and knee weaknesses.

For any possible eyesight problems, both sire and dam must pass a test by Canine Eye Registration Foundation. This group was founded by canine owners who wanted to be able to do something about the loss of eyesight of their beloved dogs. CERF testing can determine if your dog is particularly susceptible to vision problems as it ages. This is important because, as mentioned in the previous chapter, there is still no cure for retinal atrophy in dogs.

A Brain Auditory Evoked Response test can determine hearing loss. The test evaluates how a dog's external ear canal, middle ear cavities, cranial nerve, and areas of the brain stem react to sounds. BAER testing can also help determine if a dog is prone to hearing loss as it gets older.

As to possible hip and knee weaknesses, you may submit a sire or dam to testing by the Orthopedic Foundation for Animals.

If any defects or potential for defects are uncovered, the animal should be considered unsuitable for breeding.

No matter how badly you want a particular dog to be in a pairing, it's a sad fact that not all Poodles or Maltese can be suitable for producing Maltipoos.

Ideal Breeding Age

A dam Poodle should be two to three years old to be considered ideal for breeding. It is not advisable to breed a Poodle seven years or older.

Although a dog can become pregnant after the first heat, veterinarians, as well as the AKC, recommend breeding after 2 years of age, as the dog will have reached her full adult size and can now give birth with much lower risk.

For a dam Maltese, the recommended breeding age is the same.

For sires, the recommended minimum age by the AKC is eight months old.

A well-bred Maltipoo.

A Few Rules

On the side of the Poodle, only the Toy Poodle is suitable to be used for breeding a Maltipoo, not the Miniature or the Standard. Some may say otherwise that a Miniature or Standard poodle can be used to breed a Maltipoo. While this can be done, it isn't advisable because using a Miniature or a Standard Poodle will create too big a range of the resulting Maltipoo's size. This will create even more confusion where setting standard characteristics for a Maltipoo is concerned.

You are free to choose a dam or sire from either species. It doesn't make the litter any special if the dam is a Poodle, and the sire is a Maltese, or vice-versa.

However, another rule that should be followed is that the dam should be bigger than the sire. This is so that the dam will not have difficulty when it is giving birth to the pups.

Breeding for Color

As mentioned earlier, if you want a Maltipoo to come out a certain color, you must breed two dogs of the same color, and preferably have proof that the color line goes back five generations.

For example, you want to breed for a white Maltipoo, make sure you have a white purebred Poodle and a white purebred Maltese. Both must have a pedigree of only that color going back five generations.

Signs of Pregnancy

Sometimes you aren't sure if a tie was successful. Here are the signs to look out for in a dam. Both the Poodle and the Maltese dams share the same signs of pregnancy:

She is lethargic - She may want to rest more often than do the things she usually does.

Increased appetite – Since she is no longer eating for herself, but for the pups in her abdomen as well, she will consume more food.

Enlarged abdomen – Two weeks into the pregnancy, her abdomen will start to feel firm. By the fourth week, it should be noticeably swollen.

Enlarged nipples - Her mammary glands will become enlarged and noticeable. There may also be minor to moderate clear discharge, usually by the fourth or fifth week.

Frequent cleaning - She will clean herself more thoroughly than usual. This is in preparation for delivering pups.

Nesting behavior – Falling into the instinct of her wild dog ancestors, a pregnant dog will begin to gather items around the house to use in building a nest or den. These items can include pillows, blankets, and other soft materials.

The average pregnancy period for a Maltipoo is 59 to 65 days. This applies to all dog breeds.

You have the option to let your dog give birth in the clinic or at home. Dogs and their ancestors have been giving birth on their own for thousands of years, so it should be relatively safe just to watch them and assist if they appear to need help.

However, considering how important this litter is for you, you should keep your veterinarian apprised of events, starting from the time you notice the pregnancy. The veterinarian can determine if your Maltipoo is at risk of any complications, after a thorough examination.

A Warning for Maltipoo Breeders

It's ideal to breed a Poodle and a Maltese to produce a Maltipoo and stop at a first-generation Maltipoo. Breeding for second-generation Maltipoos, or having a Maltipoo tie with another Maltipoo, is not advisable.

This is for the following reasons:

Genetics - The Maltipoo is already susceptible to specific genetic defects as a result of being a crossbreed. There is no telling what weaknesses second-generation Maltipoos may have.

Aside from weakening the genes, Maltipoo owners are also against breeding Maltipoos with each other, because doing so creates a dog that isn't quite up to Maltipoo standards, and the last thing Maltipoo owners want is to muddle up the definitive characteristics of a Maltipoo. This is because Maltipoo clubs are still moving to have the crossbreed accepted as an official breed by the major kennel associations.

The size – Female Maltipoos are already very small and not designed to breed. Imagine how much one would suffer from stress if made to carry puppies.

The cost – Let's say a female Maltipoo successfully gets pregnant. She may also need a caesarian section because of the danger it poses to her health if the pups are delivered the natural way.

The risk – Veterinarians have always warned that pregnancy can be dangerous for small dogs. There will always be a chance you will lose your pet.

There is no gain to be had – While the Maltipoo is a popular breed, it has not earned enough prestige to be recognized as an official breed by any big-league kennel association. So even if you successfully produce a litter, and Maltipoo litters typically number four to five, there is no guarantee that buyers will be interested in what you have.

CHAPTER 12

Caring For Older Maltipoos

Your Maltipoo may once have been a vibrant puppy, but before you know it, it will have become an adolescent, an adult, and then a senior.

Your Maltipoo won't stay young forever, but you can do much to ensure yours has a great life!

Signs of Aging

There are signs to look out for that it has reached this stage. These can be classified into physiological and behavioral changes.

Physiological changes – The thing you may notice first is that your Maltipoo isn't that active anymore. It will want to lie down and stay there. This is because, like humans, dogs will suffer from joint pain and arthritis.

An aging dog will also have difficulty hearing. You may be surprised why it will no longer react to certain sounds, or even appear to ignore your calls.

It will also start to have eyesight problems. It may no longer react to visual stimuli like you waving a treat from a distance, a ball rolling on the floor, or animals or people passing by outdoors.

It will also experience incontinence. That means it may go pee or potty accidentally. Fortunately, for the most part, this usually happen when the animal is relaxed or lying down and not when it's moving around.

Behavioral Changes

There will also be changes in your Maltipoo regarding the way it behaves. It may seem disoriented from time to time. They may suddenly forget where the door was, or not be able to find the food or water bowl. They may even have difficulty locating you if you call them.

It may also become irritable for no reason at all, although the most likely reason for this is the pain it's experiencing from all the physical problems it is experiencing as senior dog.

Even as a senior dog suffers from hearing loss, he might still become afraid of certain noises. He might also suddenly not be able to tolerate dogs he got along well with before. He might not even be able to tell when he is in danger anymore.

There will also be other compulsive behavior like licking objects or digging at furniture.

The Daily Routine for Older Maltipoos

There were things you did every day to make sure your young Maltipoo was well-taken care of. Now that it's older, there are some things you should do differently.

Keep watch for bathroom breaks – When a senior Maltipoo goes pee or potty somewhere it shouldn't have, you should realize that it didn't do this on purpose. It simply cannot control some of its physical functions anymore.

There is even the chance it will feel ashamed after it realizes it has committed an offense, considering the years it has been trained to go outside.

Make it easier for the dog, by keeping a close eye on signs that it wants to go outside. You can also put an indoor potty patch or a pee pad in an ideal area in the house to make it easier for your dog to do its business.

Be gentler during playtime – Obviously, you can no longer play with your senior Maltipoo the way you used to when it was still younger. If the dog indicates it still wants to play, indulge it. However, it would help you not to be as "rough" with your senior Maltipoo as before.

For instance, don't pull toys as hard as you used to when they bite on it or throw the toys as far away as you once did.

Shorter walks – If your dog is still up for walks (and it will indicate if it want to do so) keep in mind that it will get tired easily now. Opt for shorter walks and in places that are easier for it to walk on.

Dog-proof the house – There was a time you made the house safe for your Maltipoo as a puppy. Now you have to make the home safe for it as a senior dog. During moments when it can become disoriented, a dog can wander into places where it can be exposed to danger, and considering dogs may lose the correct judgment when it comes to danger, they can put themselves at risk.

You can do this by putting barriers cutting the dog off from stairs or rooms with hazards like chemicals, poisons, and sharp objects. Those barriers used when the dog was still a puppy should come in handy.

Keep your Maltipoo wellfed and hydrated – While you make sure your older Maltipoo can't get to areas that it shouldn't, make sure it can find its food and water bowls easily. Keeping it wellhydrated will make sure its digestion is proper and even contribute to its energy reserves. Keeping it well-fed will make it happier.

More visits to the doctor – Of course, this is something you don't have to do every day. However, this will be something you have to do more frequently than before.

It's not just a matter of making sure your Maltipoo gets some relief from the pain it's experiencing because of its age. The fact that it's older will also mean it will start to have issues with its immune system, aside from other possible complications brought on by its age.

After all this, don't forget that you still have to bathe and groom your dog. Keeping it free from parasites is one way to make sure it enjoys the remaining time with you.

You can also make sure your dog has better food and a more comfortable bed; those years are taking their toll on the Maltipoo's bones, muscles, and joints after all.

Saying Goodbye

The sad thing is that no amount of love and care you give your Maltipoo can prevent the inevitable; it will grow old and die –or as pet lovers prefer to call it, cross the Rainbow Bridge.

So, it's best to be prepared than unprepared. There will be signs to look out for when your dog is ready to cross the Rainbow Bridge.

It will start to lose interest in everything around it and just want to lie down. It will not touch its food, it will not respond to you anymore, or any other animal or person in your family.

It will appear extremely tired, too tired to even lift its head.

Its breathing will start to get ragged and uneven.

It's likely even to poop or pee where it lays as its organs are no longer responding to its commands.

Take note that some of these signs may not mean the dog is actually dying, but suffering from an illness. These are also signs that senior dogs display as they are about to pass. In any event, please see your veterinarian.

If the signs are unmistakable and the dog's age is right, move the dog somewhere more comfortable.

There are things you can do to make the dog feel better:

Stay close to the dog – The dog may not appear to acknowledge your presence, but it will know if you are near.

Be as calm as possible – If you show distress, your dog will feel it too. You don't want your dog's final memory of you to be a wailing, sobbing mess.

If You Decide to Make a Painful Decision

Some Maltipoo owners make the decision not to let their pets suffer the pains and difficulties brought about by old age and choose to euthanize them. While we don't advise this on the outset, we acknowledge that there are some cases where this may be the best option, especially in cases where prolonging the dog's life means also prolonging its suffering.

If you have reached this extreme decision, let your dog pass the humane way. Consult your veterinarian about the most compassionate way to put down a pet, and more often than not, the likely answer will be through a lethal injection.

Make sure you and your family know everything about the procedure and what is expected to happen so that no one will feel left out.

When the time comes, it would be best if you are present when the dog passes, and that the dog knows you are there with it. It may be traumatic for you, but reassuring to your Maltipoo.

Memorializing Your Dog

There are now many ways to memorialize your dog. You can have it buried in a pet cemetery or cremated to be placed in an urn. Some dog owners tend to favor cremation so they can put the urn somewhere around the house, next to a photo of the dog during happier days. This is, of course, all your choice.

An Important Thing to Remember

This is why you have to maximize the time spent with your dog. They won't be around forever, and you know it. This isn't to say spend every waking moment with it, just make sure you are enjoying time spent with your dog to the fullest.

Take heart in the fact that throughout its life, your Maltipoo knew that you loved it and treasured it for the loyal, loving animal companion that it was.

CHAPTER 13

Further Things You Should Know

We have covered almost everything a Maltipoo owner needs to know. However, there are more things to be aware of. There's no such thing as being too informed where taking care of your pet is concerned.

Maltipoo Licenses

Some dogs require a license to own, but you don't need one to own a Maltipoo in most jurisdictions.

However, getting a license can actually be a good idea for several reasons.

If your unlicensed dog somehow escapes your yard and is found in public by an official of the city, you can face a fine of up to $250, or equivalent in your country other than the USA.

A license can help prove your dog is safe for the public. Rescuers may be wary about approaching your dog if they think it's a homeless stray.

Most importantly, dog shelters keep licensed animals longer, in the hopes that their owners will be able to come and get them. The sad fact is that unlicensed dogs are the first to be euthanized if the shelter reaches overcapacity.

If you want your dog licensed, you can do this with your city or county licensing department. You may need to present a certificate proving your dog has been vaccinated for rabies. The average license should cost between $10 to $20, or the equivalent in your currency.

Make sure the information about your dog's license is available on its collar.

Maltipoo Insurance

Again, there is no overriding law in most jurisdictions requiring that you should get your Maltipoo insurance. However, this is also advisable. In the course of your Maltipoo's life, you can never tell what will happen to it.

For most budgets, it would be more advisable to go for a plan that allows for monthly payments and lower deductibles. The earlier you have your dog insured, the better.

You will rest easier knowing that your Maltipoo in insured.

Conclusion

There is no doubt a Maltipoo is one of the best dogs you can get not just as a pet, but also as your loyal companion.

Its size makes it ideal for whatever kind of house you have, its attitude makes it suitable for children and adults alike, and its friendliness makes it the perfect companion for any other type of animal.

Do we even have to mention how cute it looks?

The process of taking care of a Maltipoo won't be a walk in the park (although sometimes this may become part of the process), and you may have your patience tried at times during training. You will also have to clean up after it, make sure it gets bathed, gets fed, stays healthy, and is groomed.

As with any task that bears long-term fruits, taking care of an animal requires commitment. There is no quitting halfway, no throwing in a well-chewed white towel.

The path to success will be marked by sweat, maybe some tears, and a whole lot of treats and worn-down chew toys.

However, you don't have to face that challenge alone. You can turn to others like your own family members, veterinarians, and like-minded dog owners for help. You might be surprised how owners of dogs are willing to help other owners and dogs as if these were their own.

If you take care of your Maltipoo, then it will take care of you in its own adorable way, making you laugh, giving you something to look at while you are bored, and offering you cuddles when you are sad.

In the end, it will all be worth it. You will have gained a loyal animal companion, unlike any other. It may be tiny, but it's willing to defend you from enemies, although it can only reach up to their ankles when it tries to bite them!

You may not be able to love a Maltipoo until the end of your life, but a Maltipoo will be sure to love you to the end of its life.

So, if you happen to have the chance to own a Maltipoo, go for it.

It's not the perfect dog, but it comes close. But while you may not think this dog is perfect, if you show the love and care which I know you will, the Maltipoo will love you back and think you are the perfect parent. All the best with your Maltipoo!

A Maltipoo can be your ideal companion for many years- Good Luck!

BONUS CHAPTER

Your Trusted Maltipoo Resource List

Here is a list of websites you might find useful for life with your Maltipoo:

Organizations that Recognize the Maltipoo:

- **North American Maltipoo/Maltepoo Club & Registry**
  http://maltipooclub-ivil.tripod.com/index.html
- **Designer Breed Registry**
  https://www.designerbreedregistry.com/
- **The International Designer Canine Registry**
  http://www.designercanineregistry.com/
- **The American Canine Hybrid Club**
  http://www.achclub.com/index.html

- **Designer mixes**

  https://www.designermixes.org/
- **Where to find/adopt/buy Maltipoos**

  https://puppyfinder.com/maltipoo-dogs-for-adoption-usa

  https://www.mydoodlemaltipoos.com/

  https://pet-net.net/dog-rehoming/maltipoos-adoption-rehoming/

  https://www.adoptapet.com/adopt-a-small-dog

  https://www.all4pawsrescue.com/adoption

  https://www.infinitypups.com/breeds/maltipoo-puppies-for-sale/

  https://www.puppyspot.com/puppies-for-sale/breed/maltipoo

  https://preferablepups.com/maltipoo/

  https://www.greenfieldpuppies.com/maltipoo-puppies-for-sale/

  https://www.lancasterpuppies.com/puppy-search/breed/maltipoo
- **Where to go for help for Maltipoo rescue (note that many of these groups also have adoption options)**

  http://maltipooclub-ivil.tripod.com/id11.html

  https://pricelesspetrescue.org/

  https://www.dreamhouserescue.org/

  https://www.all4pawsrescue.com/

  https://www.saveasmalldogrescue.org/

  https://www.peaceofminddogrescue.org/index.php

  https://www.sweetpawsrescue.org/

  https://acesangels.org/

  http://www.humaneanimalrescueteam.ca/links.aspx

- **Where to get Maltipoo supplies**

    https://www.petcratesdirect.com/

    https://www.lupinepet.com/

    https://wetdogcanvas.com/index.html

www.ingramcontent.com/pod-product-compliance
Lightning Source LLC
Chambersburg PA
CBHW070814100426
42742CB00012B/2353